# TRACING YOUR SECOND WORLD WAR ANCESTORS

**FAMILY HISTORY FROM PEN & SWORD**

# TRACING YOUR SECOND WORLD WAR ANCESTORS

*A GUIDE FOR FAMILY HISTORIANS*

Phil Tomaselli

Pen & Sword
**FAMILY HISTORY**

First published in Great Britain in 2011 by
**PEN & SWORD FAMILY HISTORY**
an imprint of
Pen & Sword Books Ltd
47 Church Street
Barnsley
South Yorkshire
S70 2AS

ISBN 978 1 84884 288 5

A CIP catalogue record for this book is
available from the British Library.

Typeset in Palatino and Optima


Printed and bound in England by
CPI UK


*Pen & Sword Books Ltd incorporates the imprints of*
Pen & Sword Aviation, Pen & Sword Maritime, Pen & Sword Military, Wharncliffe
Local History, Pen and Sword Select, Pen and Sword Military Classics, Leo Cooper,
Remember When, Seaforth Publishing and Frontline Publishing.

*For a complete list of Pen & Sword titles please contact*
PEN & SWORD BOOKS LIMITED
47 Church Street, Barnsley, South Yorkshire, S70 2AS, England
E-mail: enquiries@pen-and-sword.co.uk
Website: www.pen-and-sword.co.uk

# CONTENTS

# ACKNOWLEDGEMENTS

As ever, I owe a huge debt of gratitude to the many people who've assisted me in the course of writing and researching this book. My old friend and editor Simon Fowler, himself the author of a work on this subject, suggested me to Pen & Sword and offered help and advice; the staff at The National Archives have, as ever, been their friendly, professional and knowledgeable selves; the staff at Swindon Central and North Swindon libraries have excelled themselves in locating obscure material through the inter-library loans system; William Spencer, military expert at The National Archives, has been invaluable, as have Paul Baillie and David List, two veteran private researchers there. Bryan Clough provided very useful information on detainees on the Isle of Man and on the right-wing groups many of them came from. My wife, Francine, has been steadfast in her support and took some of the photographs.

A number of individuals must be mentioned without whom the case studies would scarcely have been possible: Sheila Meaney very kindly gave me access to her research on her late father, much of it initially done without the benefits of recently released material; my own father, Phil Tomaselli, helped me understand the relationship between our family and his cousins the Lamberts; my wife's uncle, Les Bowler, kindly loaned me his RN service record and his memoirs of naval service; Claire Stretton lent me the papers of her relative Charles Halme Rogers; Albert Rock kindly sent me a copy of his RAF service record; Steve Sparkes gave me copies of his grandfather's service record and talked to me about his life and career. Lynda Merrett loaned me her father's papers including his Ministry of Labour and National Service directive and Certificate of Gratitude.

Various other people, mentioned in the introduction, were unwitting inspirations to me through chats with them in the dim and distant past. Many I know are dead but some may still be around and may even end up reading this! This is to you gents – a pleasure to work with (and for) you and I'm glad I knew you all.

# PERSONAL INTRODUCTION

Like most people of a certain age, when I look back at my earlier life, so many of the people that I knew at school or at work had served in the Second Word War. Though most only spoke about it occasionally, I can still remember what many of them did, and little snippets of what they told me. One of my schoolteachers was a radio operator in the 8th Army; my headmaster, Harry Edwards, occasionally told us tales of swimming in the Bay of Naples or of places he'd visited while serving in 'Intelligence' in Italy in 1943 and 1944 – only recently have I learned, through an old school friend who kept in touch with him, that he actually worked for the Intelligence Corps (and possibly MI6), gathering intelligence on economic conditions in Italy and Austria.

My first employer, Ron Golding, had been a radio operator in the RAF; my second boss, John Walters, served in armoured cars and I recall him telling me how two of his best friends had been killed, in the very last days of the war, when they forgot to take basic precautions when crossing a road in Germany and were hit by machine-gun fire. Len, my supervisor in a print works, had served with 8th Army in Italy and was at Monte Cassino, one of the fiercest battles of the war, but would never talk about it. When I worked at Exeter University in the 1980s I met many men who'd served. Reg Wyatt had only joined the Territorial Army in 1938 to learn to drive, but found himself at Dunkirk in 1940 in a queue to get aboard a destroyer to take him home – instructed by a sailor to ditch his kitbag to save space, he told me he refused because it was stuffed with French silk tights he'd 'acquired', a pair of binoculars and a German officer's Luger pistol! Reg went on to drive a bus full of troops around the south coast during the 1940 invasion scare, then served in North Africa; he went ashore a couple of days after D-Day in 1944, where the men on either side of him were killed, and ended the war in Germany itself. Frank Lancaster served as a boy sailor at D-Day. Les (whose surname I don't recall) explained that he'd got two badly twisted legs because 'I was one of the first troops into Belgium in 1944 – and one of the first out again because my Jeep hit a mine just over the frontier'.

My parents were too young to have 'done their bit', but others in the family did so. Chief among these was my great-grandfather, Frederick William Lambert, who'd lost his youngest son in the First World War and who returned to sea as an Able Bodied Seaman in the Merchant Navy (he was, in fact, a ship's cook) and was killed in January 1940 when his ship was torpedoed. He was nearly 70 and my father has only a very vague memory of him pulling on his sea boots before he set out on what was probably his last voyage. My mother's uncle was captured fighting in the rearguard at Dunkirk and spent the whole war as a prisoner; one of my father's many step-uncles fought with the Royal Artillery at El Alamein. Both grandfathers were in Reserved Occupations – William Armstrong was a coal miner, but served as a Fire Watcher in Newcastle upon Tyne; Frank Tomaselli worked in the Tyne shipyards but did go to sea when vessels he'd worked on did their sea trials, including the battle-ship *King George V* on which he sailed to Scapa Flow.

Regarding so many of these people, most of them now dead as far as I know, I'd loved to have known much more. Perhaps the moral of these stories is – if your relatives who served in or lived through the Second World War are still alive, and happy for you to do so, get their memories committed to paper or recorded in some other way, for their sake, your sake, future members of the family's sake – and for the sake of posterity generally. They lived through, and took part in, momentous events. History isn't just about Churchill, Hitler, General Montgomery and all the other civilian and military leaders. They may have directed the war but it's our relatives and our ances-tors who dug the coal, built and fought in the ships, tanks and aeroplanes, fired the guns, tilled the fields and risked their lives. No history of the Second World War is really complete, at least in my book, without reference to the tremendous efforts and sacrifices they all made.

Unfortunately, with the passing of the years, there are fewer and fewer veterans of the Second World War still with us. Only a couple of years ago I visited the Army Chaplain's Museum and was told then that only a dozen or so Chaplains from the Second World War were still alive, the average age of a Chaplain having being much higher than the ordinary officer during the war.

The good thing is that information is now much more readily obtainable than it was in the 1970s and 1980s, though it is still a lot easier if you are next of kin or can obtain their permission to have information on an individual.

Many family historians will have already researched ancestors who fought in the First World War and, in principle, the methods used are the same – with the exception that, because there is a risk that the subject may still be alive, there are restrictions on access to service records so they are (rarely) available online. They can, however, generally be obtained provided you can prove to the Ministry of Defence that you satisfy their release criteria.

By using this book, you should be able to identify what types of record might be available about your relatives and will know where and how to obtain them. Some of the basic records are illustrated, with an explanation of what they contain and what information you can get from them. Following on from that you'll be able to identify the types of records that will let you follow up their service in more detail, finding out about the places they served, the kind of work they did and any actions they were involved in. I've quoted some examples of people I've helped research, using them as a guide, which will hopefully help you find out more about your relative.

# Chapter 1

# GETTING STARTED

There are some basic things you can do at the start that will make your task easier. Try and get together all the information that you already have or that you can obtain from relatives. What was your ancestor's full name? What was their date of birth? Who would have been their next of kin – their wife first usually, if they were single then usually their father or mother. Do you know which service they served in (Army, Navy or Air Force or one of the other services such as the Home Guard or Merchant Navy)? Do you know, or can you find, their service number? If they were in the Army, do you know which regiment or corps they served in? To obtain their service record you'll need to be able to provide as much information as possible to the Ministry of Defence.

What paperwork can you find – discharge papers, letters, photographs, log books, medals? Is your relative still alive, or are people who knew them and might have material or memories that might be useful? There may be information in the paperwork that will help you – a service number is ideal as every serviceman or woman had a unique number which will help the Ministry of Defence identify their surviving papers. A regimental badge, either a physical one or one that appears in a photograph, will tell you what regiment a soldier served in.

Write it all down and take photocopies of any documents that might be relevant. This avoids losing or damaging the originals. Because it can take some time to obtain service records (up to eight months in the case of soldiers) and you're no doubt keen to get started you could try simple things like searching for them by name on the Internet – you never know! There are several sites worth exploring – The National Archives (TNA) website, the *London Gazette* online, *The Times* online. If you know something of their service, i.e. which regiment they served in, ship they served on or RAF squadron they were with you can try looking for information on them.

The main archive for government records is TNA at Kew and almost any researcher will end up having to obtain information from here; there are museums on most army regiments and on the Royal Navy and Royal Air Force. The Imperial War Museum not only has extensive displays on both world wars but huge archives of donated material, an extensive library, hundreds of thousands of official photographs and film and sound archives. Local record offices will frequently have material on the Home Guard and local occurrences such as air raids. There is plenty you can be doing while you wait for service records.

## Recording Relatives' Memories

If you have any relations still living who served in the Second World War, or who remember events on the Home Front, make arrangements to talk to them as soon as possible. Always ask for permission to speak to them and explain why you're going to be asking them questions. Please remember that for some you may be asking them to recall events they'd rather not remember, things that may have happened to them, to their loved ones or their comrades in arms. Sometimes, they may have been specifically ordered not to tell people about an event and even after sixty years they may not feel free to disobey. Always bear these things in mind.

Once you've arranged the chat (don't treat it like a formal interview, you're not a journalist and it may make people feel uncomfortable), make sure you have an unobtrusive recording device (I always use a miniature tape recorder but no doubt there are more modern devices available), a notepad and several pencils. If possible, take along some memento of the period such as a photograph to act as a focus for your chat. Always ask for permission to make a recording and always check you have good batteries in your machine and are recording at a good level. Lead them into the subject gently, explain you're recording their memories for the sake of their children, grandchildren and other relatives. If they say that what they did wasn't important remind them that the big decisions of the war might have been made by Churchill and Monty but it was the work that everyone did that got Britain through.

Try and ask 'open' questions not 'closed' ones. A closed question is one that can be answered simply yes or no, such as 'Were you in the Army?' An open question is one where your subject has to open up a bit such as 'What was it like in the Army?' Let them talk, what may not seem important to you may be important to them and might become relevant later on. Don't insist they start at the beginning and go through to the end. One reason you're recording them, both on the machine and in note form, is so that you can go away and try and work out a chronology of events from what they say.

Always arrange for a follow-up chat with them a week or two later when you've had the chance to listen again to what they've said and, hopefully, devised some more specific questions. In the meantime try and do some reading up on the areas they've covered, the Blitz, the desert war, the Air Force and try and see if you can find some documents related to their service – a ship's log, an RAF station log, a local newspaper. This will prove to them that you're genuinely interested and may help spark further thoughts from them.

Talk to other surviving relatives who might know about the period. Ask them if they have any letters, photographs or documents about the ancestor you're researching. It was illegal to keep a diary (though many men did) but cameras, though not common, do seem to have been allowed. Letters were censored so that precise details of where a person was posted weren't revealed, but they may tell you that they were 'in India' or 'in the Middle East'.

## Obtaining Service Records

Service records for each of the three services, the Royal Navy, the Army and the Royal Air Force, are held in their individual record offices and the paperwork for each is slightly different. Papers for the Home Guard are (currently) held with the Army records; Royal Marine records are held by the Royal Navy; records for female members of the armed forces are held by the same record offices as their male colleagues.

The place to start is online at the Veterans Agency website: http://www.veterans-uk.info. There is a page: http://www.veterans-uk.info/recordsmedalsbadges.htm which, in turn, leads to the page for service records: http://www.veterans-uk.info/service_records/service_records.html. If you are the veteran, or if they are still alive and you are acting on their behalf or with their approval, or if you are looking for a deceased relative's papers and are next of kin or have their authority, you can go to a page you where you can download the necessary Subject Access Form.

If you are not the veteran or their immediate next of kin, or do not have their consent, it is possible to obtain a service record, but there are various restrictions because of the Data Protection Act and the Ministry of Defence's duty of care.

Under the record release scheme, and in recognition of the duty of care owed to the family of the deceased subject, for a period of twenty-five years following the date of death of the subject and without the consent of the next of kin, the MOD will disclose only: surname; forename; rank; service number; regiment/corps; place of birth; age; date of birth; date of death where this occurred in service; the date an individual joined the service; the date of leaving; good conduct medals (i.e. Long Service and Good Conduct Medal (LS&GCM)), any orders of chivalry and gallantry medals (decorations of valour) awarded, some of which may have been announced in the *London Gazette*.

After this period, and if it is held, in addition the MOD will disclose without the requirement for next of kin consent: the units in which he/she served; the dates of this service and the locations of those units; the ranks in which the service was carried out and details of Second World War campaign medals.

The charge is £30 (waived for a widow or widower). Cheques must be payable to 'MOD Accounting Officer' and should be included with the completed Certificate of Kinship and Subject Access Request (SAR) form. Obtaining records may take some time.

## Obtaining Royal Naval Service Records

From the Second World War period into the 1970s all naval personnel were given their service record when they were discharged. For pension purposes the RN only retained their pay details. Therefore, the only information held on RN personnel from the Second World War is their service details (number, rank, name etc.) and a list of dates and ships/shore bases. If your relative served in the Navy, do check any surviving paperwork you have which might be the service record – this is likely to contain more personal information about their career. If you don't have it, you can apply (if you are next of kin or obtain their authority) to: Royal Navy Disclosures Cell, Room 48, West Battery, Whale Island, Portsmouth, Hants, PO2 8DX; tel: 02392 628779 / 02392 628781. You can download the necessary forms from the Royal Navy section of the Veterans Agency website: http://www.veterans-uk.info/ service_records/royal_navy.html.

Most the Second World War Royal Marine service records are retained by the MOD and you'll also need to contact their Portsmouth office (above). If your relative enlisted before 1936, their record may be available in TNA's ADM 159 series, searchable and downloadable online at: http://www.nationalarchives.gov.uk/documentsonline.

## Obtaining an Army Service Record

Army service records are held in Glasgow. They're indexed by service number, rank, full name and date of birth – you'll need to provide as much of this information as possible, together with your relative's regiment or corps if known, to help locate them.

Records of deceased ex-servicemen/women will generally be released only to, or with the consent of, the official next of kin. You'll need to provide a Certificate of Kinship form and a SAR form, which are downloadable from the Veterans Agency website (see below). The charge is £30 (waived for a widow or widower). Cheques must be payable to 'MOD Accounting Officer' and should be included with the completed Certificate of Kinship and SAR form. Obtaining records may take some time (currently as long as eight months). The relevant page of the Veterans Agency website is: http://www.veterans -uk.info/service_records/army.html.

Address your written request to: Army Personnel Centre, Historical Disclosures, Mail Point 555, Kentigern House, 65 Brown Street, Glasgow, G2 8EX.

### The Brigade of Guards and Household Cavalry

The regiments of Foot Guards have traditionally retained their own records. Records are held by the appropriate regimental headquarters. Postal inquiries only should be addressed to: Regimental Headquarters, Grenadier/

Coldstream/Scots/Irish/Welsh Guards, Wellington Barracks, Birdcage Walk, London, SW1E 6HQ.

Records for the Household Cavalry (now the Blues and Royals Regiment but during the Second World War the Royal Horse Guards (the 'Blues') and the Royal Dragoons (the 'Royals')) are held by: The Curator, The Household Cavalry Museum, Combermere Barracks, Windsor, Berkshire, SL4 3DN.

*Obtaining a Royal Air Force Service Record*

You can obtain the necessary SAR form and Certificate of Kinship form via the Veterans Agency website at: http://www.veterans-uk.info/service_records/raf.html. The completed forms should be sent to: RAF Disclosures Section, Room 221b, Trenchard Hall, RAF Cranwell, Sleaford, Linconshire, NG34 8HB; tel: 01400 261201, ext 6711, ext 8161/8159 (officers), ext 8163/8168/8170 (other ranks).

You should provide as many details of your relative as possible, especially their service number (if you have it), full name, date of birth and rank (if possible).

*Service Records Generally*

Service records were not designed for the convenience of family historians but to provide basic details of a serviceman or woman in order to ensure that pensions, wound gratuities and medal entitlements could be worked out. They would also ensure that, in the event of recall in an emergency, the individual could be posted immediately to somewhere they could be employed – hence the listing of professional and technical qualifications and details of rank, promotions and conduct.

Hints and examples on what service records look like and how to interpret them are given in the relevant sections on each service. The records are full of abbreviations and acronyms and basic lists of these are provided in the appendices at the back of this book.

## Tips on Visiting The National Archives

Almost all the publicly released information you're going to want to look at is held are held at The National Archives (commonly referred to as TNA and formerly the Public Records Office) at Kew, including army war diaries, RAF squadron, station or other unit records, ships logs and naval reports, prisoner of war records and court-martial records. The sheer amount of information available at TNA can be daunting even for the experienced researcher and can overwhelm a first-time visitor. Before visiting, take time to look at their website which has all the basic information you'll need about getting there and what you'll need to register as a reader (at no cost).

If you've not been to TNA before, or over the last couple of years, please be aware that there have been some important changes. If going by car you may no longer be able to just turn up and park for free; as there are (repeatedly threatened and repeatedly delayed) plans meaning you'll need to register your car with TNA in advance and pay a charge of £5 per day – and you'll need to book a parking space in advance of each visit. The website (hopefully) will explain how you go about doing this, should the plans ever be finalised. You also don't need a Reader's Ticket to access what is called the Public Reading Room, which will give you access to microfilmed records and to a large number of PCs from which you can access many online sources – though to see the vast majority of Second World War records, which are still held as original documents, you'll need a Reader's Ticket to access the Main Reading Room.

There are excellent leaflets on TNA's website, which can be downloaded, on various aspects of the services and family history generally to help you in advance of your visit. Try using their online catalogue to look up documents that might be of interest by browsing the categories: AIR for Air Ministry (for the RAF), ADM for Admiralty (for the Royal Navy) and WO for War Office (for the Army) until you come to references that look promising. You can also try the 'Search' facility, which allows you to look for key words in document descriptions. Be careful – papers relating to the invasion of France on D-Day, 6 June 1944, might appear under NEPTUNE, OVERLORD, Normandy or under the codenames of any of the constituent operations on the day. Other hints on how to use the catalogue in relation to different types of record are scattered throughout this book. You may need to use your imagination and a little patience to find the documents you require. Time spent in looking at TNA's website, particularly at their catalogue in advance of your visit, is not time wasted!

Experienced family historians will already know that the more information you have when you start looking the more information you're likely to find. Don't expect to find everything on one day. Try and make a list of the most important things you want to locate first and stick to it – I know from many years experience how easy it is to get distracted! Be prepared to have to go back for more information. Obviously, the more work you are able to do beforehand in terms of looking at the catalogue and sorting out what it is you're searching for, the better and more productive your day will be. For those who struggle with online systems there are paper indexes to the records, held by reference to the department which created them (WO, ADM, AIR etc.) but the online cataloguing is improving all the time and becoming easier to use, so do give it a try.

Many documents, particularly relating to RAF squadrons for the Second World War, are available on microfilm in the Open Reading Room. You can read them and take copies. Other documents will be produced in the Main Reading Room in a cubby hole specific to your seat – which you'll need to book when you arrive, or which you'll be allocated if you order in advance.

Photocopying facilities are available or you can take digital photographs yourself, at no charge.

Don't be afraid to ask the staff for tips on to where to look. There is a very basic help point as you enter the first floor which can assist you with using the computers and can direct you in general terms where to start looking. A team of specialists, experts in the records themselves, how to find them and interpret them, is also available. Please remember that they can give you pointers and assistance – but they can't do your actual research for you! I've always found the staff to be very friendly and knowledgeable.

## Other Useful Sources

There are a vast number of other sources that can provide back-up information that will assist in your research. The Internet has a huge amount of information – just typing the words Second World War into Google produces 105,000,000 results so you'll need to try and be more specific in your search terms. Wikipedia has a very general page which gives a history of the war and a basic timeline.

You can even try just searching with your relative's name; this is unlikely to produce a result, but you never know – someone else's research may have turned them up. You can find websites devoted to individual ships, RAF squadrons and bases, military units and individual events. Some of these have been meticulously researched and are well written – I've tried to list some of my favourites at the end of the book but there are many more I keep discovering. Websites belonging to institutions are generally the most reliable in terms of the information they provide but, paradoxically perhaps, have the least information – usually because they cover a specific set of records or one particular regiment or squadron and rarely refer to individuals. Well-presented websites produced by enthusiasts often go down to the kind of level where individuals are mentioned but a word of caution is needed – whereas some of these are absolutely brilliant, specific information should always be followed up if possible using other sources.

Your local library will have a section on the Second World War and can obtain books for you using the inter-library loan service. This is a cheap and underrated means of getting rare material and one I've used with much success.

Newspapers, both local and national, can be invaluable. Your local library will usually have access to the local papers in your area – if you need papers from somewhere else then the British Library Newspaper Collection at Colindale has most of these – though at some point they propose moving to the main British Library in London, this now seems to be on hold.

Local record offices may have lots of material on local events during the war, as well as on local people, places and military units and bases.

There is a wide range of military museums, the collections of which may contain information that will help and on a good many associations relating to specific regiments, ships, squadrons or groups of individuals. While they are unlikely to have official records, they may have privately donated material or may be able to put you in touch either with surviving veterans or with their relatives.

## Access to Archives (A2A)

A2A is part of the British archives network. The A2A database contains catalogues describing archives held locally in England and Wales dating from the eighth century to the present day. Much material relating to local affairs during the Second World War, including Home Guard units, Civil Defence, local police and emergency services as well as personally donated papers, is held in local archives. A2A, accessible through: http://www.nationalarchives.gov.uk/a2a, has a search engine allowing you to trace relevant information. Just searching on 'Home Guard' produces some 2,355 references, such as the following from the London Metropolitan Archive for the Middlesex Home Guard:

This class of records of the Home Guard, comprising 4 registers and 5,432 pieces, consists of nominal rolls, superseded nominal rolls and miscellaneous documents relating to officers, non-commissioned officers and men and women auxiliaries of:

(a) 1st Battalion ('T' Zone) Middlesex Home Guard ('D' Company of this Battalion became the 4th Battalion Middlesex Home Guard).

(b) 1st, 2nd, 3rd, 4th, 5th, 6th and 7th Cadet Battalions, the Middlesex Regiment (Cadet Officers).

(c) 61st (Middlesex) Anti-Aircraft Cadet Regiment, Royal Artillery (Cadet Officers).

(d) 1st (Middlesex) Cadet Battalion, Royal Engineers (Cadet Officers).

(e) London North Eastern Railway (London) Battalion Volunteer Local Defence Corps (1940). 17th (City of London) Battalion, London North Eastern Railway Home Guard (1940–2). 33rd (Middlesex) London North Eastern Railway Battalion, Home Guard (railway and non-railway employees) (1943) (the year in brackets indicates change of title).

(f) HM Prison (Feltham) Home Guard Unit, a sub-unit of 'B' Company. 1st Middlesex Home Guard (transferred to 'B' Company on 2 December 1942).

(g) General Aircraft Ltd (Feltham), a sub-unit of 'D' Company, 1st Middlesex Home Guard (later became 9th MX. (HG) Battalion).

(h) 2nd Home Guard.

These records contain a wealth of information, not merely number, rank, and name, but personal details, hitherto unrecorded. Information includes

(a)     Full name and address.
(b)     Profession, and/or place of employment.
(c)     National Registration Identity Number.
(d)     Details of previous service in the forces (rank, branch etc.)
(e)     Next of kin.
(f)     Whether owner of a car/cycle, or any motor vehicle.
(g)     Telephone number (home or business).
(h)     Age (or date of birth).
(i)     Promotion in Home Guard.
(j)     Transfers (Regular forces, inter-unit etc.)
(k)     Discharges (through death or other causes).
(l)     Religion.
(m)     Resignation (pressure of work etc.)

Other information includes results of proficiency tests, reports upon non-commissioned officers, strength states, returns of small arms, personal history sheets, lists of category, men etc.

As you can see, this is a potential goldmine for anyone with a relative who served in the Middlesex Home Guard – and it's a reference chosen pretty much at random.

A2A also gives 286 references to Fire Watching, a key element in the Civil Defence schemes, and 3,667 references to Civil Defence itself. Glamorgan Record Office contains:

Records of the Air Raid Precautions, Glamorgan County Area, 1939–1946, consisting of: log books and attendance books relating to Glamorgan Main Control Centre, 1939–1946; Barry Control Centre, 1940–1944; Bridgend Control Centre, 1939–1945; Caerphilly Control Centre, 1939–1944; Gorseinon Control Centre, 1940–1945; Bargoed and Hengoed Control Centre, 1939–1944; Maesteg Control Centre, 1941–1944; Neath Control Centre, 1940–1944; Penarth Control Centre, 1940–1944; Pontypridd Control Centre, 1940–1945; and Whitchurch Control Centre, 1939–1944. There are no records for Mountain Ash control centre, Pentre Control Centre, Pontardawe Control Centre and Port Talbot Control Centre.

A2A allows you to search a large number of archives simultaneously, including some enormous ones such as the Imperial War Museum and is a very useful resource.

## The London Gazette

The *London Gazette is* the government's own newspaper, published daily since 1666, which lists, among many other things, military promotions and appointments (generally for officers only) and honours and awards to civilians and the military. As such it is an invaluable resource for military and family historians, although some care must be taken with it. Their online archive is available at: http://www.gazettes-online.co.uk/generalArchive.asp.

The Archive is searchable by name (or even individual words) so in theory it is possible to search for your relation's name and find out about their career and what medals or honours they were awarded, and when. There are problems with searching online – on a recent visit to the Guildhall Library they insisted I use a paper index because of the problems they'd had with online searches. If you have the service number, try searching on that first as it will produce far fewer hits than a name, even an uncommon one. Thanks to knowing his service number I was able to confirm the award of the Military Medal to No. 6398354, Corporal Wilfred Herbert Eric Goodall, the Royal Sussex Regiment (*London Gazette*, 16 August 1940) even though his service record is not released. You'll be presented with a downloadable PDF file of the edition(s) of the *Gazette* that contains the reference you are after. As ever, the more information you have, the greater the chance there is of finding out more and because of the way the search is conducted you need to be pretty exact in what you're looking for, or be prepared to experiment with combinations of full names and initials.

A useful set of tips for finding individuals (and perhaps explaining why you can't find someone you know should be gazetted) is at: http://www.military-researcher.com/LondonGazette.html.

## The Times *Online*

*The Times* newspaper (which can usually be accessed online either in your local library or via their online 24 Library Service) ran extracts from the *Gazette* almost daily, which is useful for tracing promotions and appointments of officers, but it also regularly ran extracts from the *Supplement* which contained recommendations for medals and awards. *The Times* of 24 January 1941, for example, reports the awarding of a George Cross to Ordinary Seaman Bennett Southwell and Probationary Temporary Sub-Lieutenant Jack Maynard Cholmondeley Easton, RNVR, as well as numerous other naval awards for gallantry.

It is best to use the Advanced Search section, using then the Text selection on the options provided and to keep dates fairly tight (unless searching for an unusual name). You can also restrict your search to 'Official Appointments and Notices' by clicking the options box at the bottom.

*The Commonwealth War Graves Commission*

The Commonwealth War Graves Commission (CWGC) is responsible for caring for the cemeteries and memorials of the casualties of the First World War and Second World War. Its website at: http://www.cwgc.org contains a searchable database (the Debt of Honour Register) of all the 1.7 million men and women of the Commonwealth forces who died during the two world wars and also the 67,000 Commonwealth civilians who died as a result of enemy action in the Second World War.

The search engine covers both world wars so you'll need to select Second World War as a basic criteria and from there you can search using surname, initials, year of death (if known), the force they served in – Army, Navy, Air Force, Merchant Navy, civilian or unknown, and their nationality (the site covers Commonwealth casualties as well as British ones). With limited information (for example, you may only have a name) you may find several names emerge but in most cases the reference will also produce some additional information about their family to help confirm if it is your relative.

A search under C McKay, Army, Second World War, produces five results but gives the first name, rank, service number, regiment, date of death and cemetery/memorial of each man. Checking each of them confirms that Captain Crawford McKay, 59234, Royal Engineers (attached to Inter Service Liaison Department) who died aged 30 on 11 November 1944 was the son of John and Jane R R McKay, of East Finchley, Middlesex. This is the man I was looking for.

Though the vast majority of family historians will be searching for a specific individual it sometimes pays to try and find other individuals involved in the same incident. An interesting website at: http://www.purecollector .com/history/cwgc explains how you can do this.

*Chapter 2*

# CAMPAIGN
# AND GALLANTRY MEDALS

## Campaign Medals

Almost all servicemen and servicewomen, as well as many Home Guard men and some civilians, were entitled to campaign medals, indicating where they had served. You may have their medals (which unfortunately weren't engraved with their names in the Second World War as they had been in the First World War) which will still give you some clues as to where they served. Each medal design was unique (though the stars look similar at a distance and you need to read the wording round the centre to be sure) and each medal had a unique coloured ribbon which will help you identify them. There are numerous websites to identify them: http://www.petergh.f2s.com/medals.htm, which gives good images of the ribbons and an explanation of entitlements; http://www.arbeia.demon.co.uk/srs/collect/medals/medals1.htm, which has images of the medals.

There are ten campaign medals for the Second World War, though the rules meant no individual was entitled to wear more than five. An individual with the maximum five medals was allowed a clasp to wear on one of his medal ribbons to show service that would have entitled him to another medal.

A (much simplified) list of medal entitlements is as follows:

**The 1939–45 War Medal** – awarded for all servicemen who served for twenty-eight days during the war.
**The 1939–45 Star** – awarded to all servicemen who saw active service overseas. There's a special clasp 'Battle of Britain' for members of the sixty-one RAF fighter squadrons who took part in the battle. The 1939–45 Star was the only medal awarded for service in France 1939–40, Norway, Greece, Crete and on Commando raids.
**Africa Star** – for service in East or North Africa and Malta 1940–43. There are bars for service with 8th Army, 1st Army and North Africa 1942–43. Awarded to the Army, Royal Navy and RAF.
**Air Crew Europe Star** – for all aircrew who flew over occupied Europe between 1939–5 June 1944. If they were later entitled to the France and

Germany Star, they wore a clasp on this medal instead. Awarded to the RAF only.

**Atlantic Star** – awarded mainly to Royal and Merchant Navy personnel for service in the Atlantic 1939–45, though some RAF and Army personnel were entitled.

**Burma Star** – for service in the Burma Campaign 1941–45 but not for service in Malaya in 1941, for which the Pacific Star was awarded. Awarded to all three services.

**France and Germany Star** – for service in North West Europe from 4 June 1944–8 May 1945, including Belgium and Holland. Awarded to all three services.

**Italy Star** – for service in Italy and Sicily 11 June 1943–8 May 1945, but also awarded for service between these dates in Greece, the Aegean, the Dodecanese, Corsica, Sardinia, Yugoslavia and southern France. Awarded to all three services.

**Pacific Star** – awarded for service in the Far East (excluding Burma) including Malaya and Singapore (1941–2), Hong Kong (1941) and the reconquest of Japanese occupied territory. Awarded to all three services.

**Defence Medal** – awarded for the Defence of Great Britain to all three services, the Home Guard, Civil Defence and Medical Services. Also for service in Ceylon, West Africa, Malta, Cyprus and Gibraltar.

Medals were only automatically awarded to men and women who were still serving at the time of issue. Most people had already been demobbed by this time and were expected to claim their entitlement from their service's record office. Many didn't, either through ignorance (in spite of a publicity campaign to try and get them to apply) or lack of interest at the time.

It's still possible to claim a relative's medals (or your own if you are a veteran) from the Ministry of Defence Medals Office, which handles applications from all the services. There's an explanation of exactly who is entitled to apply for medals at the Ministry of Defence website at: http://www.mod.uk/DefenceInternet/DefenceFor/Veterans/Medals/ContactingTheMedalOffice.htm; you can download the necessary application forms and supporting documentation from here.

Information and medals can only be released to the direct legal next of kin and the forms can also be used for the legal next of kin to give their permission for information or medals to be released to a different family member or family friend. You'll also need to submit a photocopy of the relevant death certificate. The completed application form should be posted to: Service Personnel and Veterans Agency (SPVA), MOD Medal Office, Building 250, Imjin Barracks, Gloucester, GL3 1HW.

There are sections dealing with the individual medal entitlements of the various military and civilian services in more detail in the following relevant chapters.

## Gallantry and Distinguished Service Awards

The main gallantry awards (**Victoria Cross**, **George Cross** and **Distinguished Service Order**) apply across all three services:

**Victoria Cross** – the VC takes precedence over all other medals, orders or awards, except the George Cross. VC awards are extremely well researched and copies of citations can often be found by Googling the recipient's name and Victoria Cross. The Victoria Cross Register is searchable online at: http://www.nationalarchives.gov.uk/documentsonline/victoriacross.asp.

**George Cross** – equivalent to the Victoria Cross for civilians, and for soldiers' gallantry when not in the face of the enemy. Introduced in 1940, it has gradually replaced other civilian awards such as the Empire Gallantry Medal, Albert Medal and Edward Medal.

**Distinguished Service Order** – awarded to officers only and usually for 'distinguished service' rather than for any particular display of heroism. Reference to the award of an 'immediate DSO' means this was awarded for gallantry. This could also be awarded, from 1942, to Merchant Navy officers for acts of gallantry in the face of the enemy.

**George Medal** – though intended as a civilian award it was also awarded to service personnel for heroism not in the face of the enemy.

### Gallantry Medals Awarded Mainly to Royal Navy Personnel

**Distinguished Service Cross** – for junior Royal Navy officers, the medal was introduced in 1901. Officers of the Merchant Navy have been eligible since 1931 and, from 1940, Army and RAF officers serving aboard ship.

**Conspicuous Gallantry Medal** – the naval equivalent of the Distinguished Conduct Medal. Rather rare – only seventy-two were awarded to the Royal Navy during George VI's whole reign.

**Distinguished Service Medal** – for petty officers and ratings in the Royal Navy for bravery in the face of the enemy, it was extended during the Second World War to cover RAF, Army, Merchant Navy and WRNS serving aboard ship.

### Gallantry Medals Awarded Mainly to Army Personnel

**Military Cross** – for junior Army officers (below the rank of Major) for gallantry, the medal could also be awarded to naval, Royal Marine and RAF officers for service on land.

**Distinguished Conduct Medal** – the oldest gallantry award to other ranks. The medal takes precedence over the Military Medal.

**Military Medal** – created in March 1916 for Army NCOs and other ranks for acts of bravery. Over 15,000 medals were awarded during the Second World War.

## *Gallantry Medals Awarded Mainly to RAF Personnel*

**Distinguished Flying Cross** – awarded to officers for acts of valour flying in operations against the enemy

**Air Force Cross** – for officers for gallantry on non-operational flights and meritorious service on flying duties.

**Distinguished Flying Medal** – awarded to other ranks, and also for Army and Navy personnel on flying duties.

**Air Force Medal** – the other ranks equivalent of the Air Force Cross.

Other ranks could also win two naval medals, the **Conspicuous Gallantry Medal** and the **Distinguished Service Medal**.

Gallantry and Distinguished Service Medals were always reported in the *London Gazette* so you can search this and *The Times* online for references. There are more details about finding out about a relative's awards in the relevant sections of the book covering the service they were in.

*Chapter 3*

# THE ROYAL NAVY

The Royal Navy was the largest navy in the world at the start of the Second World War but, even so, required thousands more officers and men as the war progressed to man the new ships necessary for anti-submarine work, convoy escorts and amphibious warfare. By 1945 the Royal Navy had almost 900 major warships and 866,000 men and women. Some 1,525 vessels of all sizes were lost in the war, including 224 large warships. Over 50,000 British naval personnel lost their lives.

One of the main commitments of the Royal Navy during the Second World War was halting German attacks on merchant ships, aimed at cutting off Britain from her Empire and Allies. These interrupted essential supplies to the home population and the armed forces. In spite of the experience they had built up in the First World War and interwar planning, the Navy struggled to counter new German weapons, such as magnetic mines and long-distance aircraft, as well as new submarine tactics, including coordinated attacks by

*Les Bowler among a group of trainee naval ratings.*

groups of U-boats known as Wolf Packs. By the end of the 1939 the Germans had sunk over 100 ships. With their capture of French ports the Germans were able to launch U-boats from a large number of bases and the Navy struggled to keep up with their expanded capability. The lease-lend of fifty old destroyers by the USA in 1940 greatly assisted in convoy escort work but the increasing sophistication of German tactics and technology meant the convoy war in the Atlantic wasn't won until late 1943 and U-boats continued to pose a threat right to the end of the war.

In addition to the convoy protection duties the Royal Navy fought in every ocean. German surface raiders, from the battlecruisers *Bismarck* and *Graf Spee* down to the cunningly disguised merchantmen such as the *Kormoran*, had to be tracked down and destroyed. In the Mediterranean there was the modern Italian fleet to face, as well as U-boats and the Luftwaffe. Amphibious operations landing small raiding parties such as Commandos and whole invasion armies had to be organised. In the Far East the enormous, modern Japanese navy and air force had to be faced and although much of the fighting fell to the Americans, they were supported by Royal Navy ships.

## Naval Service Records

*Royal Naval Officers*

You can trace an officer's basic career using the *Royal Navy List*, copies of which are available on the open shelves of TNA's Reading Room. For the Second World War these provide little information about where they were serving because the ones on the open shelves were available to the public. A top-secret set of Confidential Lists was produced, which indicate where individual officers were serving, along with the names of ships and establishments. They include a complete list of all ships in the Royal Navy, together with details of tonnage and armament. They were issued quarterly and are available in ADM 177 and can be ordered in the Main Reading Room.

Though the vast majority of service records for naval officers who served in the Second World War are retained and have to be applied for, records for the more senior commissioned and warrant officers have been released and are available online at TNA's website in the ADM 196 series at: http://www.nationalarchives.gov.uk/documentsonline/adm196.asp. The series ends with the records of regular naval officers who enlisted in 1917, so a commissioned officer would probably have to be a Commander or above for his record to be available – though you may find records of older officers who'd retired and were recalled during the Second World War. It's possible to search the records using first and last name, rank, date of enlistment and date of birth but even a search just on surname will bring up a list that can be trawled through until you find your man.

The records were created in large ledgers with, in theory, one page per officer – though for many officers, with long or eventful careers, their record had to be spread across several pages. There are also inserts containing further information. The records are largely handwritten, with quite small writing, though the scanned documents are generally quite clear. When TNA scanned the records they do seem to have ensured that all relevant pages are included so you should get a complete record of your relative's career. The record itself is generally chronological but the clerks had a tendency to cram information into gaps in the previous record (though it's usually fairly obvious) so take care when reading it.

Frederick Secker Bell was Captain of the cruiser HMS *Exeter* in the Battle of the River Plate in December 1939, when three British cruisers fought and damaged the German battlecruiser *Graf Spee* and forced her to seek refuge in the neutral port of Montevideo. HMS *Exeter* was herself badly damaged in the action but *Graf Spee* scuttled herself rather than come back out to fight. Bell's service record is online in ADM 196 because he joined the Royal Navy in May 1910, aged 12. The record has a few details of genealogical interest including his date of birth, name and profession of his father, date and place of marriage and wife's maiden name. The bulk of the record is, of course, concerned with the ships and places he served in, with notes from his senior officer on his character and qualifications. Though the record is generally chronological you have to read it carefully in order to piece together his whole career.

The record begins with his appointment as Midshipman on HMS *Cumberland* on 1 August 1914 following him through his other appoint-ments until, in March 1917, he was sent to HMS *Dolphin* to train for submarines. Following his submarine training Bell was appointed to the submarine *D6* and a note dated 28 June 1918 says 'Reported Killed' and a Special Report on another part of the record explains 'Death presumed. S/M D6 overdue & lost'. In fact, as a later note states, he'd been taken prisoner of war, was held at a camp in Karlsruhe and was released at the end of the war. On his return he immediately revolunteered for submarines.

One of his Confidential Reports from the period notes that he: 'Takes a great interest in all that he has to do. Understands men & should make a good exec-utive officer. Inclined to run up to the limit of his wine bill & fond of good living but takes plenty of strenuous exercise. Good at all games he takes up. Possesses a good physique and sense of humour.'

He continued in submarines after the war, was loaned to the Royal Australian Navy for two years in 1930 and continued to rise steadily through the ranks. He was only given command of HMS *Exeter* on 25 August 1939.

As well as details of Bell's service the record contains a number of reports on his abilities as a Captain by the Admirals under whom he served. Admiral Harwood, his senior officer at the River Plate, noted that: 'I was not particu-larly impressed by his energy or grip and would not have assessed him as much above the average.' He revised his opinion however on the basis of Bell's conduct during the battle writing:

Captain Bell had his opportunity during the battle 'off the River Plate' ending in the self destruction of the German Armoured Ship ADMIRAL GRAF SPEE. On this occasion he acted with the utmost resolution and gallantly maintained his ship in action with the enemy under difficult conditions and when his own ship had been badly damaged. Subsequently, in the repair phase in the Falkland Islands, the repair work in HMS EXETER was brilliantly carried out with no outside assistance.

Following his period commanding HMS *Exeter* he became a staff officer and was posted to the Far East where, as Chief Staff Officer, Malaya, in September 1941, he's noted as having 'incurred Their Lordships displeasure [a formal censure] in connection with the loss of MV BUFFALO by striking a mine in its proper position in No 3 minefield off Singapore'. He's noted as 'failing to ensure that suitable orders were issued and understood by those taking part in the operation'. Following the withdrawal of the British fleet to Ceylon he was responsible for developing Trincomalee as a fleet base, to the entire satisfaction of the Rear Admiral Commanding. He returned to Britain at the end of 1943, holding a variety of administrative posts and attending training courses, interspersed with periods of unemployment. He was appointed Aide-de-Camp to the King in 1947 and was finally retired from the Royal Navy as medically unfit in 1948.

ADM 196 also contains records for Warrant Officers who enlisted before the end of 1917 – these are men who reached the ranks of Gunner, Boatswain, Carpenter, Surgeons' Mate or Armourer before their discharge. Many will have continued to serve into the Second World War or may have been recalled during the war.

A general description of the records with some further guidance on where else you might find information, particularly on officers who served earlier, can be found at:

http://www.nationalarchives.gov.uk/documentsonline/adm196.asp.

### Interpreting a Royal Navy Service Certificate

A service certificate will typically contain details that will tell you all about the subject's career. In addition to their postings (the places and ships they served on) there should be information about the Port Division they served with – prior to 1956 all RN personnel were nominally in one of three Port Divisions, either Chatham, Plymouth or Portsmouth. Though in theory the Division reflected the part of the country a serviceman came from (Chatham covered London and the south east), in general terms it is unlikely to be relevant. There should also be their service number – this is unique and invaluable in checking whether a man mentioned in official documents is your relative – particularly if he has a common name. Letters in front of the number indicate the branch of the Navy they served in – the letter J indicates

| Name | BOWLER | Leslie Frederick George | | | |
|---|---|---|---|---|---|
| Name of Ship. (Tenders to be inserted in brackets) | Substantive Rating | Non-Substantive Rating | From | To | Cause of Discharge and other notations authorised by Article 606, Clause 9, K.R. and A.I. |
| Collingwood | Ord Sea | | 13 Oct '43 | 31 Dec '43 | |
| Valkyrie | | | 1 Jan '44 | 30 Jan '44 | |
| Pembroke | | | 31 Jan '44 | June '44 | |
| Swiftsure | | AIRC 3 | 2 June '44 | 12 Sep '44 | |
| — " — | Able Seaman | R.C. 3 | 13 Sep '44 | 9 Dec '46 | |
| Pembroke | — " — | — " — | 10 Dec '46 | 7 Feb '47 | Released Class A |
| | | | | | 9576 - |

*Part of Les Bowler's service record showing the ships to which he was appointed.*

Seamen and Communications, for example, and the letter K indicates a Stoker.

The period of service indicates whether they were a Regular or a Conscript. If an ancestor was a 'Regular' there will be a time period entered here – for most Second World War naval personnel there will be references similar to 'Entered under the National Service (Armed Forces) Acts', i.e. a Conscript.

Medal entitlements will tell you what medals they were awarded before they were discharged. In most cases these will only be campaign medals. Please note that other medals might have been claimed later so will not appear on the certificate, which was issued on discharge.

The section of the certificate entitled 'Wounds, Meritorious Service, Prize Money and other grants' details whether a man who'd been wounded was paid a wound gratuity and if there were awards for meritorious service or prize money, which could be paid to someone who'd taken part in the capture or sinking of an enemy vessel. In most cases there is only a war gratuity and post war clothing grant ('demob suit').

The excerpt from Les Bowler's certificate shown above details his various postings during his career. Please note that every RN shore establishment was also a 'ship' so will also appear here. If the ship's name appears in brackets then the relative was posted to a tender – which was a support ship, possibly for a submarine flotilla, trawler flotilla or other small ships. Much of their active service might have been on one of these vessels rather than on the tender itself.

Les Bowler was called up in 1943 and given a limited choice of which service he wanted to be in. He chose to be a Seaman in the Royal Navy and was formally called up in October 1943 and posted to HMS *Collingwood* for basic training. After further training to become a radar operator he saw active service on the new cruiser HMS *Swiftsure*, where he was a radar operator, working the Identification Friend or Foe (IFF) system that identified friendly

*HMS* Collingwood, *RN Training Establishment, drawn by Les Bowler.*

aircraft. Serving in the Pacific, he visited Australia and New Zealand, saw action with the 4th Cruiser Squadron as part of Task Force 57 of the American Fifth Fleet, shelling Japanese island positions and covering the landings at Iwo Jima and Okinawa. Here he saw kamikaze attacks and *Swiftsure* herself suffered a near miss from a bomb. After Japan's surrender *Swiftsure* was among the first British ships to return to Hong Kong and then proceeded to Nagasaki, where Les was able to visit the remains of the city less than two months after the atomic bomb had been dropped.

Details for Les Bowler's postings show that he was first posted to HMS *Collingwood* in Fareham, which was commissioned in early 1940 as a new-entry training camp for hostilities-only ratings. His second posting was to HMS *Valkyrie*, which was a training base for radar operators. He was next posted to HMS *Pembroke*, which was a shore establishment at Chatham but was also used for accounting purposes as a nominal posting for pay purposes. His final posting was to a real ship: HMS *Swiftsure* was a light cruiser, the first to be fitted with the latest radar and fire-control systems for anti-aircraft defence. She served with the British Pacific Fleet in 1945. Her Ships Logs are in ADM 53 between 120599 and 124650.

Once you have the service record, particularly the list of ships served on, you can begin to look for records that will allow you to find out more about what your ancestor actually did. Because so many Royal Navy ships were, in fact, nominal ships, I've tried to prepare a list of these stone frigates (land bases or permanently moored ships), which appears in Appendix 1.

## Operational Records

Over the last few years a determined effort has been made by TNA to index the ADM series records covering the Second World War, the majority of which, relating to ships, individuals and activities, are in ADM 1, ADM 116 or ADM 199 series. The indexing has been done by the title of the file, so provided what you're interested in occurs in the title you can search online at TNA website.

I was doing some research on a man who served, for part of the Second World War, on HMS *Grenville* and a simple search on 'Grenville' restricted to ADM and the years 1939 to 1945 produced a range of results, including her surviving log books in ADM 53, a report on proceedings from 1939 (ADM 1/10166) and some material on changes in signalling practice as a result of HMS *Grenville*'s experiences (ADM 1/10718). It was only when checking that I realised that the original Second World War HMS *Grenville* had been sunk by a mine in January 1940 (Wikipedia is helpful in relation to this kind of thing) and that the HMS *Grenville* I was looking for had been built in 1942 and was a U Class destroyer.

I was then able to find what I particularly wanted – ADM 1/12488 – describing a night fight in the Channel in October 1943 in which HMS *Grenville* and six other RN vessels were ambushed by German torpedo boats. HMS *Charbydis* and *Limbourne* were sunk and *Grenville* was missed by a torpedo by just 5ft. The recommendations of HMS *Grenville*'s Captain, about how to avoid future ambushes, explained the course of the action and the lessons to be learned.

Unfortunately, searches like this do not often turn up much material. Most ships served in larger formations such as flotillas, task forces or fleets. There are a series of index cards at TNA which offer some hints, especially to records in the ADM 199 series.

## *The ADM 12 Series*

More detailed indexing, including references to individuals and ships, are held in large ledgers in the ADM 12 series. Each year is likely to have several volumes, indexed alphabetically. Each page is divided into three sections dealing with 'Officers', 'Ships' and 'Promiscuous' (meaning miscellaneous). Knowing the name of the person, ship, place or subject you're interested in you can use the index to trace mentions of them, with a further reference to the actual document in one of the other series. ADM 12 is invaluable for locating references to individuals, especially regarding awards they had won.

Though each volume is indexed alphabetically this is only in as far as each ledger divides up into sections starting with the first letter and then the second letter, i.e. La, Le, Li, and within each subsection entries are chronological, though the clerks, having started a reference for HMS *Leopard*, would try and keep all entries for that ship together. This means that there can be quite a lot of information to wade through before any particular entry is reached. Where individuals are concerned it may be wise to search the entire volume in case there is (accidentally) more than one entry.

Having located the references for the ship or individual you're looking for you now need to find out what each individual reference means and where

*HMS* Swiftsure, *British cruiser and Les Bowler's ship.*

to access the document. Please be aware that not all individual documents survive. If the reference is prefixed with WH (War History) then the following number is usually the Case Number in ADM 199. It's also often possible, given the general sub-heading, to use TNA's search engine to locate relevant papers. Several of the references to HMS *Swiftsure* refer to either Task Force 57 or Operation Iceberg and searching these on the catalogue produces numerous useful results. If there's no WH prefix then the papers are most likely to be in the ADM 1 series, which is absolutely enormous. If a search under the subject you are looking for on TNA's search engine turns up nothing (and it is unlikely to do so when searching for individuals, especially regarding medal awards) there is a 'Packing List' for ADM 1 on the open shelves where you can use the original reference number to locate the current ADM 1 reference.

There's a guide to using the ADM 12 series available online at TNA website at: http://www.nationalarchives.gov.uk/records/research-guides/admiralty-index-digest.htm and it will repay careful reading before attempting to use the series. Even so, you may well need to take the advice of TNA staff to decipher the ADM 12 reference and turn it into a reference in the other series.

## Registers of Deaths of Naval Ratings

ADM 104/127–ADM 104/139 contain registers of deaths of naval ratings between September 1939 and June 1948, arranged alphabetically (ADM 104/127 covers A–Blyth) giving name, service number, branch of service, rating, ship's name, date and place of birth, cause and place of death.

## The Royal Naval Museum

The Royal Naval Museum at Portsmouth covers 1,000 years of naval history including much on the Second World War and on the WRENS. Their website

*The crew of HMS* Swiftsure *celebrating the crossing of the equator en route to the Far East.*

at: http://royalnavalmuseum.org has search facilities for their collections and links to other useful sites and collections.

## Ships Logs and Movements

Ships logs are in ADM 53 at TNA and you can search for them in the online catalogue using the ship's name. Usually they only record the ship's movements and weather conditions with the briefest description of any action the ship might have been in so are of little use for researching individuals. I was able, however, to get the exact date of my wife's uncle's visit to Nagasaki in 1945 by consulting the ship's log for HMS *Swiftsure* – which also confirmed that members of her crew had made a tour of the ruins only a fortnight after the atomic bomb had been dropped.

One word of warning – log books for ships smaller than a cruiser (destroyers, corvettes, frigates) don't seem to have survived – and of course final logs of ships sunk in action went down with them.

Ships' movements can be traced using ADM 187, the Pink Lists, which were printed at regular intervals and show the locations and movements of Royal Navy ships of all types, including those of the Reserve Fleet, Fleet Air Arm units and ships of Allied countries.

ADM 208 contains the Red Lists, again printed regularly, which show all the minor war vessels in home waters under commands and include the vessels of Allied countries.

ADM 209 lists ships under construction and ADM 210 lists landing ships, craft and barges in home waters and foreign stations under the commands they served in.

## The Submarine Service

If your relative served aboard submarines their service records (obtainable through the Portsmouth office) may not show which individual submarines they served on, because ratings were sent to Depot Ships as part of a pool of trained personnel for a submarine flotilla. The archive of the Submarine Museum at Gosport holds the surviving Movement Record Cards for ratings from the First World War to the end of the Second World War showing the individual submarines that men were assigned to. Submarine Log Books are held at TNA in the ADM 173 series. ADM 236 series contains an incomplete set of reports of British submarines, mostly relating to Mediterranean waters.

The RN Submarine Museum website at: http://www.rnsubmus.co.uk details opening times, location, special events and collections. A brief history of the service and complete list of submarine losses is available at: http://www.rnsubmus.co.uk/general/losses.htm#a1.

## The Fleet Air Arm

The Fleet Air Arm (FAA) flew the ship-based aircraft of the Royal Navy and went into the Second World War with six operational carriers though only one, the *Ark Royal*, was a truly modern ship.

The FAA served in every naval theatre of the war providing air support to the fleet. In 1940 FAA aircraft carried out the first successful dive-bombing attack on the German cruiser *Konigsberg* and sank her in Bergen harbour and FAA aircraft fought during the whole Norway campaign. During the Battle of Britain twenty-two FAA pilots were rapidly retrained on Spitfires and Hurricanes and loaned to the hard-pressed RAF. In addition, two FAA squadrons, 804 and 808, took part in their Skua and Fulmar fighters. A total of nine FAA pilots were killed during the battle.

In the Mediterranean, twenty-one FAA 'Stringbags' (as the Fairey Swordfish biplanes were affectionately known) attacked the Italian Battle Fleet in its home port of Taranto on 11 November 1940. As a result, 3 Italian battleships were severely damaged and the fleet crippled, for the loss of 2 men killed and 2 captured. In the North Atlantic aircraft from HMS *Victorious* and *Ark Royal* were crucial in crippling the *Bismarck*. For a large part of the war in the North Atlantic the FAA flew anti-submarine operations for the vital convoys that kept the nation supplied.

FAA pilots and aircraft carriers served in the Indian Ocean and Pacific against the Japanese. HMS *Hermes* was sunk off Ceylon in 1942. In 1945, as the tide turned against Japan, FAA aircraft carried out their largest ever air raid against oil refineries at Palembang on Sumatra, and other carriers and aircraft supported American operations against Okinawa and the Japanese mainland until her surrender in August 1945.

At the end of the Second World War the FAA had 52 operational carriers and 3,243 pilots and had earned its place as a permanent arm of the Royal Navy.

Service records for FAA personnel should be applied for via the Royal Navy Disclosures Cell, Room 48, West Battery, Whale Island, Portsmouth, Hants, PO2 8DX; tel: 02392 628779/02392 628781. At TNA, FAA squadron records can be found in ADM 207 and AIR 27 and there are some log books of RAF men who served with them in AIR 900. Individuals and ships, as well as specific operations, can be searched for via TNA's search engine or by using ADM 12.

The Fleet Air Arm Museum at Yeovilton contains much information about Air Arm aircraft and squadrons, including some material that mentions individuals during the Second World War. They are based at RNAS Yeovilton in Somerset and their website, which explains how to contact their archive, is at: http://www.fleetairarm.com.

The Fleet Air Arm Archive at: http://www.fleetairarmarchive.net/home.html is an independent website devoted to the Arm with much excellent material.

## Royal Marines

The Corps of Royal Marines are soldiers who serve at sea and are part of the Royal Navy, though their officers are listed in the *Army List* as well as *The Royal Navy List* and they hold Army ranks. By the Second World War the Corps had somewhat lost its role; detachments of Marines served on most ships for use in landing parties and on major ships they manned a gun turret, but when the first amphibious warfare Commandos were formed in 1940 they were Army formations and the first Royal Marine Commandos weren't formed until 1942. In 1943, 40 and 41 RM Commandos participated in the Sicily invasion and seven (42 to 48) other Commandos were formed. On D-Day five Commandos were in the initial landing, with other Marines manning landing craft, support units and bombarding ships. 4th Marine Brigade cleared the Schelde estuary allowing access to Antwerp. Other units fought in the Mediterranean and Far East. Some 80,000 Marines served altogether during the Second World War and the Corps had its own artillery, and engineers.

As Royal Marine officers have the distinction of appearing in both the *Royal Navy List* and the *Army List* this makes tracing the basic facts of their careers easier. Records of a few senior Royal Marine officers are available online in TNA's ADM 196 series, though an officer would have had to have enlisted in 1917 so would probably be a Lieutenant Colonel (or possibly just a Major) at the start of the war to be included.

Once you have their service record you can begin to trace either the ships they served on, if they were serving afloat, by searching for its name in TNA's catalogue or by referring to the ADM 12 records. Royal Marine units, like their Army counterparts, kept war diaries and most of them are in TNA's WO 202 series, which includes war diaries of the Royal Marine Division, Special Service and Commando Units, Training Units, Mobile Naval Base Defence Organisations etc., and despatches, letters and reports and files on operations. Some Royal Marine Commando war diaries may also be found in DEFE 2, records of Combined Operations Headquarters, which include, for example, war diaries of No. 1 (RM) Commando from October 1943 to 30 September 1945 in DEFE 2/48.

The Royal Marines Museum website at: http://www.royalmarinesmuseum.co.uk details some records in its archive. It also provides a useful factsheet, which includes information that will help you understand the various forms that comprise a Marine's service record and details the type of material they hold that might help family historians.

## The Royal Naval Reserve (RNR) and Royal Naval Volunteer Reserve (RNVR)

The RNR consisted of Merchant Seamen and officers who'd given a commitment to transfer to the Royal Navy in the event of war. Many were fishermen who were sent to man anti-submarine or mine-clearance trawlers. Others served on board merchant ships which were armed and acted as escort vessels for convoys. The RNVR was made up of men, not necessarily with sailing experience, who were called up or volunteered in wartime.

Service records for officers are to be found in ADM 240 and ADM 340. Many naval officers in the Second World War served temporary commissions in the RNVR and their records may have to be applied for through Portsmouth. For RNR ratings, the service records (which were held in card form) are in microfiche form in BT 377/7. The cards each represent a five-year period of service so do expect to have to look for more than one card for any man. The cards can be searched both by name and by number and they do cover National Servicemen. The records run as late as 1955 and the originals are held at the Fleet Air Arm Museum at Yeovilton (see above for details).

BT 164/23 lists RNR Officers: awards, casualties, deaths, prisoners of war and missing. It is available online and can be searched.

## Courts Martial

Courts Martial are military courts that try military personnel for crimes against both military and civil law. Charges cover relatively minor ones such as drunkenness (which seems to have been particularly popular among naval officers) and insubordination through to murder. It was standard for a naval officer to have to undergo a Court Martial or Court of Enquiry over the loss of their ship so you may need to search for a Court of Enquiry on TNA website.

There are some papers relating to Courts Martial in ADM 1 series, though most are procedural. There also some in ADM 116 and ADM 178 but you may need to search with a ship's name for these as individuals aren't always mentioned by name.

ADM 156 series comprises cases and files extracted from ADM 1, ADM 116, ADM 137 and ADM 167 from 1890 onwards. They contain records of Courts Martial of officers and men of the Royal Navy, Royal Marines and the Naval Reserve and Auxiliary Forces. Records for the Second World War period are between ADM 195 and ADM 266 and cover only very serious charges. You can search by name with the usual warning that occasionally only one defendant is named, the rest being described as 'and others'. If you're lucky enough to find a relative's record (though the survival does indicate they faced a serious charge) you should get the trial transcripts as well as the evidence and finding and sentence.

If you can't find a Court Martial mentioned in any of the above categories it's still possible to find some details by looking at ADM 194 series which contain Courts Martial registers of the Portsmouth and Plymouth Divisions and several overseas battalions of the Royal Marines. The Second World War period registers are between ADM 194/278 and ADM 194/301; they're divided into records of trials of officers and records of trials of Petty Officers, Seamen and Royal Marines. These registers give basic details of the individual, their ship, the charges and the finding and sentence.

*The entire ship's company of HMS* Swiftsure.

# Women in the Royal Navy

In 1939, as part of a programme to 'Free a Man for the Fleet', the Royal Navy began recruiting women to act as cooks, clerks, despatch riders and in intelligence. The Women's Royal Naval Service (WRNS – quickly dubbed 'Wrens') expanded rapidly and Wrens were soon working as radio operators, meteorologists, bomb range markers, with a few even going to sea as cypher officers, coders and boat's crews. At their peak, in September 1944, there were 74,000 WRNS officers and other ranks serving in the Navy.

Wrens worked at shore stations all over the world, many of them far from the sea. At Bletchley Park, where the Government Code & Cypher School broke enemy codes, the majority of the thousands of women staff were Wrens, involved in the code-breaking programme, acting as radio operators, Morse code readers and teleprinter typists. Postings to Bletchley may appear as GC&CS but possibly also SLU (Special Liaison Units), FSIU (Field Signals Intelligence Units) or GCHQ (Government Communications Headquarters).

The Queen Alexandra's Royal Naval Nursing Service (QARNNS) served in troop ships, hospital ships and land hospitals around the world.

Service records for the WRNS and QARNNS were, as with their male colleagues, handed over to the individual when they left the service but a basic record can be reconstructed and you'll need to contact the Royal Navy Disclosures Cell in Portsmouth. Once you know their postings from the record provided you can try and trace records of the bases they worked at.

The Royal Naval Museum at Portsmouth (http://www.royalnavalmuseum.org) has a specific WRNS collection which was transferred to the Museum from the Director of WRNS Office in 1987. It has been supplemented with private donations and transfers of material, and includes approximately 5,000 items encompassing photographs, manuscript items, artefacts, uniform, paintings and drawings relating to the WRNS during the First and Second World Wars, as well as the Permanent Service from 1947–93 when the WRNS became integrated fully into the Navy.

*Case Study – Terry Meaney, AB RN JX303000, POW 27085*
*Stalag VIIIB, Lamsdorf*

Sheila Meaney always knew that her father had served in the Second World War and that he'd been a prisoner of war, but he was not a man given to talking about his experiences. Over the course of many years she picked up several clues: 'One thing though that he was resolute about was "Dieppe Day". From my earliest memory, to the day of his death, he always "remembered" 19 August.' From occasional conversations over the course of many years Sheila knew that her father had been stationed at one point at Hayling Island in a former holiday camp ('The holiday camp scarred him forever – He would never go to Butlins even though as a 10 year old it was my heart's desire'). She also knew that he'd crashed a landing craft on the beach at

Appledore in Devon, that he'd done some training at Loch Fyne ('swimming there was the coldest thing he'd ever done') and that he'd been on the Dieppe raid, been wounded, treated by the Germans at a hospital in Rouen and sent to a POW camp at Lamsdorf.

As well as the anecdotal information she'd collected Sheila had a few bits and pieces – a newspaper cutting saying that Terry was a Commando, was in the Royal Navy and was 'missing' at Dieppe, some photographs taken at Stalag VIIB, a small book detailing names and addresses and lists of food and cigarettes sent from home, the name HMS *Astrid* and, most precious of all, a taped interview that her father did not long before he died for his grandson's school history project. This is more than many people have to start out with, but Sheila was keen to find out a lot more about the unit her father served with and what he was doing at Dieppe.

Sheila's first task was to obtain a copy of her father's service record from the MOD section in Portsmouth that provides them. Unfortunately, the record, when it arrived, made no mention of Dieppe – indeed he seemed to have slipped effortlessly from HMS *Quebec*, the Combined Operations Training Centre at Inverary, to HMS *Drake* (POW). Sheila was disappointed: 'The "ship" that was assigned to him on 20 August was his POW "posting" and there were no details of where he was taken prisoner or where he spent the rest of the war. So there was no record of his presence on the Dieppe Raid or official notification that he spent three years in Lamsdorf.'

Sheila sensibly went back to her original sources. Her Nan had saved the newspaper cutting from the *Bristol Evening Post* describing Terry as both Royal Navy and as a Commando and stating that he'd been taken prisoner at Dieppe. She set about researching the raid itself and it was clear from his recorded memoir that he'd not been part of 3 and 4 Commandos which landed at Dieppe and he'd always said he went ashore with the Canadians. Her father had once mentioned climbing the cliffs at Eype near Bridport and the local museum confirmed that on pre-Dieppe exercises these had been used by the Royal Regiment of Canada for practice. She wrote to the Royal Regiment's historian to see if they had any records of British personnel landing with them and

*Terry Meaney among a group of fellow prisoners at Stalag VIIB.*

received 'a very sharp reply stating that no British troops were involved'. This only made Sheila even more determined to prove her father's participation.

Commando Terence Edward Meaney (20), R.N., 56, Liminster Av., Knowle, is reported missing from the Dieppe raid. An old boy of 'Holy Cross School, Bedminster, he worked for Messrs. Josiah Williams, silversmiths.

She placed an advertisement in the *Bridport News* asking for any eye-witnesses to the Dieppe exercises in the area. She was contacted by Les Hawkins, who'd been on the raid himself as a member of a signals regiment. He gave her a book, *Dieppe August 19th 1942 – Combined Services Commemorative Roll.* Inside the cover it

*A press clipping announcing that Terry Meaney has been posted missing.*

read 'Personnel of the allied forces and civilians who were involved in the most disastrous seaborne raid of all time'. With trembling hands she turned to the section naming those who had died, were missing, had been captured or died in captivity. In spite of trying every variation of her surname Sheila was unable to find mention of her father. She did find a reference to Private Frederick Englebrecht who was a prisoner at Stalag VIIb and who she knew was a friend of her father, which was some encouragement – as did a note in the Roll which said 'To compile a list of participants is a long, arduous process, considering the large number of servicemen who took part and the reluctance of the Ministry of Defence to give any ungazetted information except to immediate next of kin . . . it is recognized that this listing is not complete'.

In searching through the 6,000 names Sheila did begin to notice occasional references to Royal Naval Able Bodied Seamen being killed, wounded or captured as part of beach parties. Looking up RN beach party online produced references to a body called the Royal Naval Commando. This began to sound promising and with some assistance from me she was able to track down some documents at TNA. ADM 199/1079 'Operation "Jubilee": plans, reports and appreciation' included 'Most Secret Orders for Beach Parties' and showed that the Canadians at Blue Beach had three designated officers and four men attached. Another document, DEFE 2/328 '"Jubilee" Part 3' included a description by Captain G A Brown of landing on Blue Beach with three naval ratings, one of whom, a signalman, was wounded as soon as they landed. Was this a reference to Terry Meaney? A final document, written in 1946, from the Beach Commando HQ to HQ Combined Operations says 'Attached are accounts of each Commando. Some of them unfortunately are sketchy, as a great deal of our historical records appear to have vanished in a monumental spring clean we once had.' At least here there is an explanation of why early records of the Beach Commandos are incomplete.

A later release of the Prisoner of War Questionnaires in WO 344 (see section on Prisoners of War) in Terry's own handwriting provided poignant proof of his wounding and capture on the Dieppe Raid.

# Chapter 4

# THE ARMY

pproximately 3,800,000 men and women served in the Army during the Second World War, the biggest of the armed forces. The Army came under the overall organisational control of the War Office – hence its records at TNA come into the WO series. To the average soldier the most important factor in his service was his regiment or corps – corps were mainly the support troops (though they could and did take part in fighting and the Royal Armoured Corps were a fighting unit per se), such as the Royal Engineers, Royal Army Service Corps, Catering Corps or Royal Corps of Signals. Most corps troops served in numbered companies and you'll need to know which company an ancestor served in to trace their career. Regiments were the fighting troops – cavalry, who had almost all become armoured troops by 1939, fought as regiments numbering between 800 and 1,000 men; infantry fought in battalions of about 800 men belonging to regiments which, with the exception of the Guards Regiments, were county based, i.e. the Norfolk or Wiltshire Regiments. Each regiment raised several battalions which were numbered – you'll need to know which battalion an ancestor served in to trace their career.

At the beginning of the war the Army consisted of the Regular Army, professional soldiers who enlisted for a set period in a full-time military role and the Territorial Army (including the Yeomanry Cavalry, most, but not all, of whom were now armoured units), part-time soldiers liable to full-time service in the event of war. With National Service and the rapid enlistment of hundreds of thousands of new soldiers, the distinction soon broke down. There was rapid modernisation following the defeat in France in 1940 and units that had previously been infantry or cavalry became motorised infantry, anti-aircraft artillery, signals, armoured or coastal artillery units.

As in the First World War, the fighting troops were organised into divisions comprising headquarters, supply, communications and support troops, along with the fighting units themselves, the artillery and either tanks or infantry (though every armoured division would have some support infantry and every infantry division some armoured fighting vehicles). The war diaries are collected at TNA by the theatre that was served in and grouped together under the division in which the units fought.

# Finding Your Army Ancestor

## Officers

Even without a service record it's possible to find some basic information about an officer's career using the *Army List*. These are the monthly lists prepared by the War Office detailing the records of officers (please note that other ranks do not receive any mention). Before about 1938 they'd tell you what unit an officer served in, and where it was. It was finally realised that these lists (which could be purchased from HMSO quite openly) could give the enemy a huge amount of information. As a result the lists were changed so that only details of promotions were given. If your relative served before 1938 as an officer they will be extremely useful, otherwise they will tell you nothing more than the service record will. Large libraries may have copies of the list and your local library may be able to find copies. With reservations, because of the difficulty in finding material, you can also use the *London Gazette* online to trace promotions.

## Army Service Records

To obtain the best and most comprehensive information on an individual you will need to approach the Army Records Office at Glasgow (see Chapter 1). There is a considerable waiting list for them to produce information, currently (October 2010) about eight months, though as Second World War records did not suffer in the Blitz as First World War records did you should eventually receive material.

The information you'll receive from Glasgow is not a simple summary of your ancestor's service and postings. It consists of a variety of separate records which can be difficult to read and understand. You'll have to combine the details from several record sheets and cards to create your own chronology. Glasgow provides a list of Army abbreviations to help you decipher the abbreviations and acronyms that appear on the records. I've provided two similar lists of Army abbreviations in Appendices 2 and 3 which may also assist.

Surviving records generally comprise forms or cards summarising general correspondence. These contain some genealogical information (date of birth, details of spouse, next of kin) but mostly deal with postings, service abroad, injuries or wounds and conduct.

A variety of forms or cards may be sent to you including enlistment documents (Army Form B284) which may contain brief records of service, Regimental Conduct Sheets (recording disciplinary offences like drunkenness or overstaying leave), Medical History and Dental Treatment Sheets. Of greatest use in tracing service is the Service and Casualty Form (Army Form B103). This gives basic personal information, then details promotions (acting temporary, local or substantive), appointments, transfers, postings, attachments etc., forfeiture of pay, wounds, accidents, admission to and discharge from Hospital, Casualty Clearing Stations etc., date of disembarkation and embarkation from a theatre of war (including furlough etc.). The whole basic structure of the soldier's career is here.

There may also be an Army Form B102 which contains similar information to the B103, but usually in more condensed form. There may also be discharge papers providing some details of where they served, along with a testimonial (brief written note by an officer saying how they conducted themselves).

Don't expect to find anything about what the unit your relative served in was actually doing – for this you'll need to consult their war diary. The service record should provide enough information to help you trace the relevant diary/ies.

## Case Study – Interpreting a Form B103: Frederick Thomas John Sparkes

Fred Sparkes joined the Army Reserve in May 1938 aged 23. The Reserve committed a man to six months of basic training and then regular training, while remaining a civilian. He was called up for active service on 2 September

*Three images of Fred Sparkes' service record and Service and Casualty Card showing his postings.*

# SERVICE AND CASUALTY FORM (PART I).

Army Form B 103—Part I.

Army No. 459033 W     Signature of Officer _____ OFFICER i/c R.A.O.C. RECORDS

| | Corps | Unit |
|---|---|---|
| Surname SPARKES | R. A. O. C. | No 1 O.R.C. |
| Christian Names Frederick Thomas John | | No 1 B.O.D. |
| Religion C of E | | 35 A.O.D. |

If married state date 1st · 11 · 1936
*Substantive Rank & Appointment   CPL
*Acting, Temporary or Local Rank,   L/Sgt
   giving date. B.285.
Attestation paper
(Number of Army Form)
If of Alien origin state particulars
Date of birth as declared on attestation 1· 8 · 1915
(a)
Date of Enlistment 19 · 5 · 1938
Date Service reckons from
(b) Date called to Colours
Period of Engagement 4 years
(c) Special conditions (if any) of
  Enlistment or Rate of Pay
(d) Any subsequent variations
  of conditions of service
Extension of Service
(Dates and period to be stated)

Date of Re-engagement _____ Period ____ yrs.
Trade on Enlistment Storeman
Corps trade and grade Clerk I
Qualifications (e) Tp Tech
Miscellaneous entries (f):—
(f) (1)
(f) (2)   O.S. 8/82
(f) (3)   RELEASE GROUP 22 c
(f) (4)

To be completed by O. i/c Records when the Soldier is transferred
  to or re-engaged in the Army Reserve :—
(i) Date of transfer to Army Reserve
(ii) Rank on transfer to Army Reserve
(iii) Date of promotion thereto
(iv) Service in present rank ____ Yrs. ____ Days.
(v) Re-engagement or Re-enlistment for Sec. D Army Reserve
  Date _____ Period ____ yrs.

Medical (b)

| Category | Date | Authority |
|---|---|---|
| B 3 | 23/8/40 | |
| A.1. | 25.2.45 | |

* Full Name and Address of Next of Kin and Relationship.

Continued beyond 21 years to _____ (date service expires)

NOTES.—* Entries to be made in pencil.
(a) Here enter particulars of any subsequent claim as to actual age after verification by birth certificate.
(b) Instructions regarding completion of this sub-head will be issued when necessary after mobilization.
(c) Whether "for Home Service only," enlisted at special rates of pay, &c.
(d) If to be retained on Home Service, period, if specified, to be stated, also authority, and on what grounds.
(e) Signaller, Farrier, &c.
(f) Instructions regarding allotment of these sub-heads will be made as may be necessary after mobilization.

| (A) No. of Part II Order or other Authority | (B) Unit | (C) Record of all casualties regarding promotions (acting, temporary, local or substantive), appointments, transfers, postings, attachments, &c., forfeiture of pay, wounds, accidents, admission to and discharge from Hospital, Casualty Clearing Stations, &c. Date of disembarkation and embarkation from a theatre of war (including furlough, &c.) | (D) Place of Casualty | (E) Army Rank | (F) Date | (G) Service not allowed to reckon for pension Yrs. | Days | (H) Signature of Officer certifying correctness of entries |
|---|---|---|---|---|---|---|---|---|
| G. Branch | 1st Ord Railhead | Attd C. of I. in Railhead Ord Duties for period 19/8/42 to 22/8/42 Result:- 57% Classification Q2 | Carlton | Cpl | 22/8/42 | | | Marshall |
| Pt II 224 17.9.42 | Arnold | Promoted A/U/Cpl within the estab. W.e.f. 22/8/42 Granted acty pay R.W. W.e.f. 22/8/42 | Arnold | Cpl | 30/9/42 | | | |
| Pt. II 8/3 d/21.11.42 | 10.R.H. Coy | Granted War Substantive Rank of Cpl W.e.f. 20.11.42 having held acting rank for 90 days | Chinstone | do. | 20.11.42 | | | |
| | " | Embarked for serving overseas | Field | " | 25/11/42 | | | |
| ...02£... | " | Disembarked M.E.F. N. Africa | Field | " | 6/12/42 | | | |
| Pt II 10/43 | " | Posted to No 1 B.O.D | N Africa | " | 1·2·43 | | | |
| Pt II 17/2k d/23.43 | " | Amend entry Pt II 10 d/17.2.43 to read | " | " | 1·2·43 | | | |
| | " | Posted to X (iv) List No 1 Q.B.D | " | " | 1·2·43 | | | |
| X List Pt II 14/30 d/13.3.42 | 1GBD | SOS X (iv) List (1 G.B.D) on posting | " | " | 1·2·43 | | | |
| | " | to 1 O.R.C | " | " | | | | |
| XPt II 2k/21 d/7.5.43 | " | Reclassified Clerk Tech Class I | " | " | 23·4·43 | | | |
| X Pt II 31/25 d/9/6/43 | " | Posted 'x' (ii) List on admission to 96 G Hosp. | " | " | 22·5·43 | | | |
| X Pt II 31/43 d/9/6/43 | X (ii) List | Disch. from 96 G Hosp. to X (iv) List (5 Bn 1 GBD) | " | " | 24·5·43 | | | |
| 187/44 | 500 AOD | To S. from X (iv) | " | " | 28·10·43 | | | |
| 105"/44 | 500 AOD | Awarded Africa Star | " | " | 12·4·43 | | | |
| 478 W | B. AOD | To S. from 500 AOD | " | " | 6·3·44 | | | |
| 1092/44 | 35 AOD | T.o.S. 35 AOD | " | " | 6·4·44 | | | |
| | " | Adm. Hos. S.O.S. to X (2) | " | " | 24·5·44 | | | |
| 1266/44 | " | T.o.S on disch | " | " | 29·5·44 | | | |
| — | 35 AOD | To S from 500 AD Bn | " | " | 30·5·44 | | | |

1939 as part of the Royal Army Ordnance Corps, the part of the Army that supplied munitions and equipment to the rest of the Army.

His Service Record contains a series of Service and Casualty Forms detailing his career, but because he served in more than one theatre of war and was in hospital, and because war diaries in the Second World War are organised by theatre of war or type of unit, it can be difficult to identify the specific units he was attached to. There's a list of how war diaries are organised at TNA in the section on war diaries. By diligent searching it's possible to identify the specific posting by unit so you can locate the individual diaries. You can use TNA's website to search for specific units using their numbers, but in some cases you may have to go wider.

Fred Sparkes was attached to No. 7 Ordnance Store Company (war diary in WO 167/905) and on 26 September 1939 disembarked for France where he was temporarily attached to Headquarters of No. 1 Sub Area (Cherbourg) Assistant Director Supply and Transport (WO 167/77). He was admitted to No. 4 General Hospital (WO 177/1113) and then posted to No. 1 Base Ordnance Depot (WO 167/1168). He was evacuated to Britain on 6 July 1940 and posted to Didcot, which searching under WO 166 (Home Forces War Diaries) show was the Central Ordnance Depot (WO 166/5365). From here (and this doesn't show on his Form B103 but is on a separate form on his service record) he was posted to the Ordnance Sub Depot at Olympia (WO 166/5353) and in April 1941 to 60 Section RAOC (WO 166/5370).

In August 1942 he was posted to 1st Ordnance Railhead at Carlton and then to Arnold – this required a Google search to discover that there were large Ordnance Corps depots at Carlton and Arnold just outside Nottingham. He was posted to No. 1 Railhead Company (WO 166/9658) with whom he embarked for service overseas on 25 November 1942 and disembarked in North Africa on 6 December where his unit war diary becomes WO 169/12265. In North Africa he was posted to No. 1 BOD (Base Ordnance Depot) (WO 169/6103). He was admitted to 96 General Hospital (WO 177/1370) and then to 500 Army Ordnance Depot (WO 169/12172). He had a two-month spell in a Motor Transport Stores Company (MTSC) and with 500 Army Ordnance Depot (WO 170/2752) before being posted to 35 Advanced Ordnance Depot (WO 170/2749 and WO 170/2750 for 1944 and WO 170/6282 and WO 170/6283 for 1945). He embarked for Britain on 5 September 1945 and on his return was posted to the ROAC Depot and Holding Unit (WO 166/17393) and then to 14 Battalion ROAC (WO 166/17366) from which he was discharged from the Army on 7 December 1945.

You'll note that even a Corporal in the RAOC served in many units throughout his service – also that, as he served in Britain, in North Africa and Italy and spent time in hospital, you'll need to check four sets of war diary collections (WO 166, WO 169, WO 177 and WO 170) to locate all the relevant war diaries.

# War Diaries

All Army units kept a war diary that recorded their activities on a day-by-day basis and these are invaluable for finding records of movements, training and actions that an Army ancestor took part in. The war diaries are held at TNA (though the regimental museum will usually hold a copy) but are held by the theatre (or part of the world) that the unit was in. It's possible, therefore, that if a unit served in the Expeditionary Force to France in 1939, then in Britain after Dunkirk, was sent to North Africa and later served in France after D-Day that you'll have to search several theatres to piece together the unit's whole history.

## *War Diaries by Theatre of Operations*

| | |
|---|---|
| War Office Directorates (including Intelligence, Personnel, Operations), the 'Head Office' departments in London | WO 165 |
| Home Forces | WO 166 |
| British Army in France/Belgium 1939–40 | WO 167 |
| British Army in Norway 1940 | WO 168 |
| Middle East (North Africa, Sicily and Italy 1941–3) | WO 169 |
| Central Mediterranean (Greece and Italy 1943–6) | WO 170 |
| North West Europe (France, Belgium, Holland, Germany 1944–6) | WO 171 |
| South East Asia (India, Burma, Malaya 1941–6) | WO 172 |
| West Africa | WO 173 |
| Madagascar | WO 174 |
| North Africa (Tunisia and Algeria 1941–3) | WO 175 |
| Smaller Theatres (West Indies, Iceland, Gibraltar, Russia and island garrisons) | WO 176 |
| Medical Services (i.e. Hospitals and Ambulance Units) | WO 177 |
| Military Missions (to Allied forces) | WO 178 |
| Dominion Forces (Australian, Canadian, New Zealand and Indian forces) | WO 179 |
| Home Guard units (unofficial diaries and histories) | WO 199 |
| GHQ Liaison Regiment | WO 215 |
| Special Services (i.e. Special Forces – SAS, Commandos, SBS, Long Range Desert Group etc.) | WO 218 |
| Royal Marine Commandos | DEFE 2 |

It's always worth bearing in mind that almost every Army unit was part of a larger formation – infantry battalions were generally grouped into brigades, which were then part of a division, for example, and to get a bigger picture of what a unit was doing it is often worth looking further up the command chain and examining their war diaries to find out more of the context of what was going on.

## What War Diaries are Likely to Contain

Every Army unit was required to complete a war diary. For infantry battalions this was done at battalion level but for support corps such as the Royal Army Ordnance Corps or Royal Engineers, which tended to operate at company level, diaries were compiled by company. The diaries were standard and reasonably free format so that on quiet days there is likely only to be a line or two, perhaps even 'Nothing unusual to report', but other days can take up several pages, particularly when the unit was in action. There are four columns, the first three recording Place, Date and Hour and the fourth, much larger column, headed Summary of Events and Information. It's in this last column that events of the day are recorded.

In addition to the day-to-day events the diary will usually contain a certain amount of other documentation such as copies of Orders, either for exercises the unit was to take part in or for actual fighting. There are also likely to be Returns of Officers which will tell you which officers were with the unit at a given time, some Returns of Other Ranks which unfortunately only list numbers rather than names, occasional notes of other ranks who are absent (which does mention names) and lists of other ranks transferring in or out – which does give names. Very occasionally there will be narratives written by a senior officer that elaborate on events – there's an interesting narrative in the war diary for 6th Battalion, Duke of Wellington's Regiment, sent to Iceland as part of the occupying force in 1940, which describes conditions in Reykjavik. It reports the reluctance of local girls to be seen with British troops, the high prices and the problem of the cinema films not finishing until after the end of the troops evening pass. The narrative also notes 'Although the men protested about the price of beer and its extremely poor quality they continued to drink it so fast that in a very few days there was no beer left in the town.'

When the unit was in action, the tone of the diary changes. The diary for 2nd Battalion, the East Yorkshire Regiment, which went ashore on D-Day, is light on detail for the very earliest stage of the assault, though it notes 'The assault Coys sailed past and were cheered by the remainder of the Bn who were waiting to be loaded.' Once the Colonel and Battalion HQ got ashore the diary begins to contain more detail:

Some difficulty experienced in negotiating the underwater obstacles in the increasing swell but on the whole the beaching was very good. Cross fire and sniping was fairly considerable and accurate enemy Mortar and shell fire was causing some casualties. The difficulty of evacuating casualties was increased by the rapidly rising tide, fire, and the fact that the M.O. was hit on disembarking . . . D Coy lost their Coy Comdr when a mortar bomb burst among the Co H.Q. and some difficulty was experienced in collecting them.

The diary goes on to explain the difficulties caused by marshy ground and enemy fire and that:

R Gp [reconnaissance group] in moving to a position from which to make a suitable recce was caught by a salvo in a sunken lane. Lt Col C.F. Hutchinson was hit in the arm and in the absence of Major G.W. Field who was collecting the track vehicles on the beach the command passed temporarily to Major S.R. Sheath. The attack on DAIMLER was put in by A & C Coys supported by 76 Fd Regt and was quickly secured for little loss. Some 70 P.W.s of the Arty Coastal Btn surrendered and considerable enemy weapons were captured of 4 x 7.5 cm several 40 mm AA guns and numerous small arms.

The battalion's Bren Gun carriers, mortars and anti-aircraft guns had now come ashore and the battalion moved to defensive positions and dug in. The diary for 7 June confirms their casualties for what had been a hard day's fighting – 5 officers and 60 men killed and 4 officers and 137 men wounded, with 3 men missing.

By using the war diaries it's possible to get a reasonably thorough idea of what your ancestor went through. The Army did have several squadrons of aircraft for close cooperation with the Royal Artillery – Army officers were trained as pilots and observers – these units have Operation Record Books in the same way as RAF units.

## Case Study – Why Fred Sparkes Never Trusted Officers: An Ordnance Corps War Diary (France), 1940

Fred Sparkes, according to his family, was always suspicious of officers, as he considered that he'd been abandoned by them during the chaotic retreat from France in June 1940. His Service and Casualty Forms state that he was posted to No. 1 Base Ordnance Depot and their war diary from 1 June–20 June 1940 is in WO 167/1168.

The diary does reflect the chaos that occurred when the Germans broke through the front line and began moving south into the British back area. For the first fortnight everything seems to have proceeded normally – the diary records problems with unloading trucks because of mixed loads, though on 7 June it reports '138 trucks were unloaded yesterday This is the highest number we have dealt with so far in one day. We are fortunate in having so many railheads.' There are mentions of occasional air raids and of strengthening the defences of the depots against possible parachute attacks but it's only on 15 June that the diary records 'Conference at Headquarters. Commander noted that evacuation order had been received and we were to aim to clear out in 48 hours.' On 16 June evacuation to the docks was proceeding, but:

All roads very crowded with refugees and progress to docks very slow. Best progress in this respect being made at night . . . Report received that mouth of river and river have been mined by enemy during the night. Stores may now have to be shipped via St Nazaire or at a port south of Nantes, nothing definite decided.

By 1430 hours on 16 June there are definite signs that things were breaking down as the diarist (Colonel G W Palmer) was receiving contradictory orders and struggling to locate men who could drive his heavier vehicles:

I then contacted Lieutenant Colonel Suggate and found that he had only been left with sufficient personnel for his own use. I asked Lt Col Suggate if he knew what arrangements had been made as regards duties of OC, ROAC Nantes sub area. He answered that he knew of none. Then contacted Area HQ to ascertain latest position and was informed that there were doubts whether any MT or store ships would get up to Nantes.

Palmer then suggested and received approval for the movement of all transport to St Nazaire and began moving men and vehicles in that direction.

By early morning of 17 June communications were breaking down – the Nantes Docks telephone exchange had been disabled by the operator – and lorries were backing up. Palmer began giving orders for the destruction of stores and equipment, for motorcycles and other transport to be disabled and for the removal of the breech blocks of artillery guns held in storage. Desperately trying to find men to carry out his orders (there were some 600 tons of stores at Nantes Docks that needed destroying) Palmer discovered that at least one unit he'd hoped to use had apparently begun to withdraw contrary to orders.

At 1145 hours Palmer received orders to move himself and all remaining personnel to the docks at St Nazaire. On the way to the docks he discovered groups of men without officers and convoys of abandoned vehicles:

Proceeding along St Nazaire road I found a number of workshop machinery lorries ditched. No officer present, but from enquiries made it appears destruction of the whole of this convoy was carried out under the orders of Captain Blackman RAOC of No 4 Ports Workshop detachment. Vehicles were ditched on the main Nantes – St Nazaire road causing considerable congestion of traffic. No NCO had been left with this party and all the valuable machinery appeared to be intact.

On arrival at St Nazaire the roads were congested with troops and guns of all descriptions and the town was under air attack.

Among the chaos of the docks he found Captain Blackman:

who was standing with his party waiting to embark. I asked him why he had abandoned his machinery lorries on the Nantes road near Savenay. He stated that when he arrived at St Nazaire that morning an officer of Movement Control had instructed him to return to Nantes as there was no crane capable of lifting above 3 tons at St Nazaire. Asked why he had not carried out these instruction he said that he had met a sergeant of the Military Police who said that it was no good returning to Nantes.

Desperately trying to sort out which of his valuable vehicles he was to try and get aboard ship for evacuation to Britain, Palmer called at the HQ Movement Control to speak to Brigadier Gill, telling him: 'I did not know where I was, there being so many orders and counter orders and that it was necessary for me to receive definite and final instructions otherwise it would be too late'. Poor Gill was unable to give him any clarification: 'He had just received information of the sinking of the liner *Lancastria* with 6,000 men on board and it would seem probable that all available shipping would be required for personnel, that he had heard that there were not many survivors and that it had just been reported that 50 enemy planes were on the way.'

Sending his driver, chief clerk and despatch rider to get some tea Palmer had a brief dinner with Brigadier Gill (who said he'd not eaten for twenty-four hours) and dossed down in the chateau gardens: 'Too tired to sleep, but lay there in a very depressed state at the thought of that terrible spectacle of so much abandoned military material which all and sundry had worked so hard to try and get away. It was not long before enemy planes were over us again and the bombardment started.'

At 0220 hours next morning Palmer was roused with the news that it still might be possible to get some of his vehicles aboard ship, but investigations showed that there were still no cranes capable of lifting them aboard. Troops covering the evacuation were pulling back closer to the town and the RAF was threatening to withdraw what little air cover they'd been able to provide. Inspecting the edge of the town Palmer 'found guns in position with ammunition lying around the guns. majority of vehicles ditched and guns had had breech blocks removed – a heart breaking sight – all along the roads were abandoned vehicles, some ditched, some run up into side lanes, leaving desolation everywhere'.

Convinced that there were now very few troops still to be embarked, Palmer returned to Brigadier Gill, who informed him that German troops were now thought to be only two hours away. Collecting his Chief Clerk, Sub Conductor A J Howes, his driver Lance Corporal Bardsley and his despatch rider, Private Davis, Palmer embarked on a small boat and was picked up by the SS *City of Lancaster*. At 1015 hours the ship set out, in convoy, for Britain, accompanied by the sound of heavy anti-aircraft fire directed at German aircraft.

They eventually arrived in Britain on 20 June and Palmer gave his men forty-eight hours leave before reporting himself to the War Office recording that he was 'worried as to the number of men I may have had on the ill fated *Lancastria'*.

Fred Sparkes' Service and Casualty Forms merely record that he was 'Evacuated to UK' at this time. Fortunately he wasn't one of the men on the *Lancastria*. His low opinion of officers seems however to have been justified – though many were undoubtedly individually brave they seem to have lost control of the situation, forcing troops to have to make their own decisions if they wanted to get away.

## Army Courts Martial

Courts Martial are military courts that try military personnel for crimes against both military and civil law. The vast majority of Court Martial offences were relatively minor ones such as drunkenness, absence without leave or theft, though personnel could be tried for much more serious offences such as murder or treachery. Records for actual Courts Martial for 'minor' offences are unlikely to have survived, though it should be possible to find some details.

Registers of Courts Martial for the Army are in TNA's series WO 213 and are all available for the period of the Second World War between WO 213/35 and WO 213/65. The series is divided into ledgers for Field Courts Martial and Military Courts at home and abroad, so you'll need to know if they were in Britain or abroad and the date of the trial. The left-hand page of the ledger records the details chronologically, but by the date that the results were received in London, not necessarily the date of the trial. It could take some months for the result to be recorded (I've seen examples where trials held in November were not recorded until the following April or May). You will get confirmation of name, rank and regiment, so you can be sure you're looking at the right person. The location of the trial is usually just listed as 'In field' with a note of which theatre. On the right-hand page there will be the nature of the charge, which is by type of offence rather than the specific charge itself and then the sentence.

Records of Courts Martial for the more serious offences (murder, treason, mutiny, cowardice, aiding the enemy etc.) are in WO 71 series, between WO 71/691 and WO 71/1001, which is, in part, searchable by the name of the defendant. Unfortunately, in some cases only the name of the principal accused is given, for example, WO 71/940: 'Sparrowhawk, F. and 30 others Offence: Mutiny.' Once again it will help if you have a date for the trial. Records in WO 71 generally include a transcript of the trial itself, along with photographs and copies of the evidence. You may find some files are still listed as 'This document is closed and cannot be viewed or reproduced as a digital or printed copy.' It is possible to request a review of the file closure using the Freedom of Information Act and the catalogue reference gives you a link in order to do this. There's no requirement for you to provide an explanation in your application and you should hear back from TNA within twenty working days, though they may require additional time to consult other departments (they'll advise you of this).

## Army Gallantry Awards

It's possible to look for Army recommendations for medals and awards for the Second World War online in TNA's WO 373 series. Unfortunately, as their website says, 'It is unusual for files relating to honours and awards announced prior to 1950 to have survived; those that have are included here.'

Citations cover a huge range of honours and awards: the Victoria Cross, George Cross, Order of the Bath (GCB, KCB and CB), Order of the British Empire (GBE, KBE, CBE, OBE, MBE), Distinguished Service Order, Military Cross, Distinguished Flying Cross, Military Medal, George Medal, British Empire Medal, Mention in Despatches, Distinguished Conduct Medal, Royal Red Cross, Burma Gallantry Medal and Indian Order of Merit.

There are, among others, 16,809 citations for the Military Medal, 11,614 for the Military Cross, 2,759 for the Order of the British Empire and 4,009 citations for Mentioned in Despatches.

The search facility is quite extensive, allowing you to search for an individual by first name, last name, rank, service number, unit, theatre of operations or award – so it's a useful tool for researching units and types of medal as well as just people.

I was delighted to find the citation for my old headmaster's MBE. I knew he'd worked in Intelligence in the Mediterranean Theatre and had been awarded an MBE, but not what for. His citation, from Allied Force Headquarters, gives his name and regiment, Harry Garner Edwards, Lieutenant (Acting Captain), Intelligence Corps and reads:

> Has been in charge of I9 (x) in First Army and latterly A.F.H.Q. since the start of operation. He is outstanding in his work and has changed the I (x) organisation at A.F.H.Q. from a state of disorganisation to one of efficiency. He has the confidence of all officers of A.F.H.Q. and of officers at formations. I consider that his work undoubtedly merits some recognition.

With many of the recommendations for gallantry awards the citation will usually include enough detail of the action to allow you to find the unit war diary so that you can look at the fighting in perspective.

## Women in the Army

### The ATS

Hundreds of thousands of women served during the Second World War, including Her Majesty the Queen who, as Princess Elizabeth, trained as

Driver in the ATS. Conscription was introduced for women in 1941. In the Army they generally served in the Women's Auxiliary Territorial Service (ATS) as clerks, drivers and mechanics, in radar stations and decoding units and operated anti-aircraft guns. In June 1943 there were 210,308 officers and women in the ATS. Their service records are in the same Glasgow MOD office as their male counterparts.

Most ATS served on attachment to other units so you'll need to find the war diaries from the units they served with, though there are some war diaries specific to ATS units throughout the main series. You can search on TNA's catalogue using Auxiliary Territorial Service as the key search term.

The Women's Royal Army Corps Museum collection has passed to the National Army Museum, Royal Hospital Road, Chelsea, London, SW3 4HT; tel: 02077 300717; website: www.national-army-museum.ac.uk.

## First Aid Nursing Yeomanry (FANY)

A small volunteer organisation created before the First World War, the FANY formed the basis of the first ATS Motor Driver Companies. Other FANY were attached to the Polish Army. Many FANY joined the Special Operations Executive (or were commissioned into FANY as cover) serving as cipher clerks, radio operators and administrative assistants. Many of SOE's women agents were FANY.

Records of FANY members are at their HQ: FANY (PRVC), TA Centre, 95 Horseferry Road, London, SW1P 2DX. A charge may be made for finding records.

## Nurses and the Voluntary Aid Detachment (VAD)

The Army nursing service was provided by Queen Alexandra's Imperial Nursing Service. Service records are held by the MOD in Glasgow. A few hospital war diaries are available at TNA. A specific medal awarded to military nurses is the Royal Red Cross. There are registers for awards covering the Second World War in WO 145/2 and WO 145/3. Medal citations are in WO 373.

The VAD were part of the Red Cross, running hospitals and convalescent homes as well as helping staff military hospitals, acting as support staff to nurses, administrators, ambulance drivers and cooks. Their service records are held by the Red Cross in the form of record cards, information on which may include dates of service, the nature of duties performed, the detachment belonged to, the institutions and places where they served and any honours awarded.

For access to information, write to the Museum and Archives Department, British Red Cross, 44 Moorfields, London, EC2Y 9AL, providing as many details about the individual as possible. In particular, it's useful to include: any known addresses, middle names, maiden or married names, date of marriage, any known service details and date of birth. Though no formal charge is made for information, a donation would be gratefully received.

## Other Sources for the Army

### The Army Roll of Honour

The Army Roll of Honour is a list of Army servicemen and servicewomen who died in the Second World War. The list gives details of rank, regiment, place of birth and domicile (by town, county or country) and theatre or country where the fatal wound was sustained or death occurred.

There's a hard copy of the Roll of Honour in TNA's WO 304 series which is listed alphabetically so you can call up the relevant section of the Roll. It is unlikely, however, to provide anything more than you'll find on the Commonwealth War Graves Commission's Debt of Honour website and there are online versions (for a fee) at: www.military-genealogy.co.uk and http://www.ancestry.co.uk.

### Regimental Museums

Army museums hold a wealth of general information on their respective regiments. Army Museums, Ogilvie Trust is a registered charity that assists military museums, with a website at: http://www.armymuseums.org.uk. The site allows you to search for regimental and corps museums that may have useful information. Once located the site gives links to the museum's website, details of its location and facilities.

The websites themselves differ considerably in terms of the amount of information they have immediately to offer. The Museum of The King's Own Royal Lancaster Regiment (website at: http://www.kingsownmuseum .plus.com) gives concise histories of each of the Regiment's battalions; the Museum of the Royal Engineers (http://www.remuseum.org.uk/ index.htm) includes access to online pamphlets regarding specific technical aspects of the Corps' work and a large section that deals with the work of the Engineers in the many campaigns in the Second World War. It includes the following testimonial from Field Marshal Montgomery who said, after the war:

> The Sappers really need no tribute from me; their reward lies in the glory of their achievement. The more science intervenes in warfare, the more will be the need for engineers in the field armies; in the late war there were never enough Sappers at any time. Their special tasks involved the upkeep and repair of communications; road, bridges, railways, canals, mine sweeping. The Sappers rose to great heights in World War Two and their contribution to victory was beyond all calculations.

Though every museum's collection is unique it's usually possible to make some generalisations. They'll usually have copies of the war diaries – so if they're close it may not be necessary to visit TNA to look at these. Most museum archives also hold extensive collections of photographs, donated material such as personal diaries and letters, copies of the *Army List* and copies of orders. The Lincolnshire Regiment archive, now held at the Museum of Lincolnshire Life, part of which houses the Regimental Museum, can provide an eighty-page listing of their holdings, including:

392. Records relating to Private John George Elliott.

John Elliott was born on 25 July 1918. John Elliott enlisted in the Militia in 1939 and served in the regular Army during the Second World War.

Soldier's pay and service book 1939–1945.

Ration book 1941.

Photograph of the 4th Battalion of the Lincolnshire Regiment in Utrecht shortly after liberation 1944.

Line-up for a friendly football match between the Lincolnshire Regiment and some young Dutch men undated [c. 1944].

National identity card 1943.

Soldier's release book 1945.

(Museum accession/reference numbers: 392)

and:

808. Diary of events compiled by officers of the 2nd Battalion of the Lincolnshire Regiment.

Covers the period from mobilisation to the evacuation of the British Expeditionary Force from Dunkirk August 1939–June 1940.

Also includes notes compiled by Brigadier T G Newbury MC immediately after returning from Dunkirk. Covers the period from 29 August 1939–29 May 1940.

(Museum accession/reference numbers: 808)

Museums also have a large collection of books specifically related to their regiment and the actions they took part in which will certainly give you an idea of books you can obtain from your local library.

It is always worth contacting museums in advance, particularly if you want to look at their archives as they usually have only a skeleton staff, most of whom are volunteers, and limited access to material as a result.

## The National Army Museum

The National Army Museum in Chelsea is the museum specifically dedicated to the Army as a whole. As such it's unlikely to hold material relating to a specific individual but it has extensive collections of photographs and a large library. The museum website is at: http://www.national-army-museum .ac.uk and there is a page dedicated to people researching soldier ancestors at: http://www.national-army-museum.ac.uk/oldResearch/researchTips .shtml.

## Tracing Former Army Comrades

The Royal British Legion runs a service called 'Lost Trails', which aims to reunite old Army friends. Contact Legionline by telephone on: 08457 725725 to register your search on this computerised service, or write to Legion, Centurion Publishing Ltd, 17 Britton Street, London, EC1M 5NQ. You can also register at: www.forcesreunited.org.uk.

*Chapter 5*

# THE ROYAL AIR FORCE

At the height of the Second World War some 110,000 Officers and 1,050,000 other ranks were serving in the Royal Air Force (RAF). On the outbreak of war the RAF had 157 squadrons with nearly 2,000 front-line aircraft, though only 270 were Hurricanes and 240 Spitfires. RAF units fought in every theatre of the war, including squadrons sent to Russia to protect the ports used by the Arctic convoys. Fighter squadrons defended Britain against the Luftwaffe in the Battle of Britain, bombers attacked enemy targets, including the huge and costly campaign against German cities and industry, and Coastal Command helped the Royal Navy against enemy U-boats in the Atlantic.

## Where Your Ancestor Fitted into the RAF

Whereas Army personnel joined a regiment or corps, each a part of the Army, RAF personnel joined the RAF itself and could be posted to several squadrons or stations during the course of their service. Squadrons undertook operations and stations were bases for one or more squadrons, and housed the men and supported and coordinated their work. The RAF also had many support units including technical schools, hospitals, depots and repair bases to which someone could be posted, and even had its own soldiers for defence of these bases – the RAF Regiment, formed in 1942 (see below).

In the Second World War the RAF was organised into commands according to specific roles. Initially these were Bomber Command, Fighter Command, Coastal Command and Training Command. On 1 April 1938 Maintenance Command was created, followed by Balloon Command on 1 November that year. Training Command separated into Flying Training Command and Technical Training Command on 27 May. Army Co-operation Command was created on 1 December 1940 (and disbanded on 1 June 1943). Ferry Command was formed (from Atlantic Ferry Organisation) on 20 July 1941 and then became Transport Command on 25 March 1943.

Control of the RAF came under the Air Ministry so papers at TNA are in the AIR series. Once you know from an individual's service record their squadron(s), station(s) or unit(s), and the dates they served there, you can begin to look for the records that will tell you more about what they did. Whereas the Army has war diaries, the RAF has Operation Record Books

(ORBs) which detail their day-to-day activities. AIR 27 series holds squadron ORBs, AIR 28 station ORBs and AIR 29 ORBs of the many small units (such as Air-Sea Rescue units, training schools and maintenance units). You can search for the relevant ORB(s) using TNA website's search facility.

Each unit came under a command and each command had its own structure, squadrons and/or RAF stations. It was, however, quite possible that an individual serving in the RAF would serve in more than one command during their career, especially if they were an officer, as their career progressed.

As they are the highest levels of RAF organisation papers, the commands are extremely unlikely to contain information immediately relevant to the family historian but they will be an invaluable source for planning and policy papers for certain operations or reports of incidents.

The command papers are grouped in TNA series:

| | |
|---|---|
| Balloon Command | AIR 13 |
| Bomber Command | AIR 14 |
| Coastal Command | AIR 15 |
| Fighter Command | AIR 16 |
| Maintenance Command | AIR 17 |
| Overseas Commands | AIR 23 |
| Air Training Command | AIR 32 |
| Ferry & Transport Command | AIR 38 |
| Army Co-operation Command | AIR 39 |

## RAF Service and Service Records

As a technical service the RAF required recruits to undergo a huge amount of training. Pilots spent many months learning to fly (frequently in Canada, the USA or South Africa), then various familiarisation courses into the types of aircraft they'd be flying and pre-operational training. The same applied to navigators and other aircrew. Ground crew didn't necessarily require quite the same level of training but many of them were also specialists in aircraft repair and maintenance, radar and radio equipment and working with engines. The first year, at least, of an RAF recruit's service would have been taken up with instruction and there would be frequent training updates during the rest of it.

Unlike the Army, the RAF collated information on a serviceman's career into one document, which at least means that everything is in one place. This is a Form 543A which provides basic personal information such as name, service number, date of birth, civil occupation, next of kin, details of marriage (if any) and a physical description.

In terms of their RAF service it shows details of their date of enlistment, date of release, promotions, special qualifications, Good Conduct Badges received and, perhaps most importantly, the stations and squadrons they were posted to. This is the complicated bit – unlike the Army, where a man tended to be posted to one regiment or corps for his whole career, in the RAF (and this applies to the Women's Auxiliary Air Force as well) the individual joined the service and was then posted to a series of reception and training centres and schools, then would probably serve in a series of squadrons or bases as their career progressed. As a highly technical service the RAF referred to these on the service record by a series of initials which can be hard to understand at first; a basic list of these abbreviations is provided in Appendix 4.

Along with the Form 543A the service record may include a copy of the Royal Air Force Certificate of Service and Release. As well as confirming basic details of service, including dates of any service overseas and medal entitlement there's usually a brief reference to an individual's service and to any particular aptitudes for future employment. The certificate (for Wireless Operator Albert Rock) reads: 'Is returning to pre war employment as wages clerk. Has initiative and administrative ability, is conscientious and hard working.' It is always pleasing to read testimonials such as this about one of your relatives.

## Establishing Information on a Career from Online Sources: A Work in Progress

I received the service record for Sergeant Eric Hall having no previous knowledge of his service. Using the list of RAF acronyms in Appendix 4 and TNA's

| Dep. P.O.R. | Unit From | Unit To | Reason | Check'd. | Appd. | Date of Movmnt. | P.O.R. confirmg. Arrival. | Occ. M. Qtrs. |
|---|---|---|---|---|---|---|---|---|
| | | 2RC | | | | 29.4.43 | | |
| | 2RC | Res. | | | | 30.4.43 | | |
| | Res | 1 ACRC | | | | 20.9.43. | | |
| 243/43 | | 21.1TU | | | | 9/10/43 | | |
| 99/43 | | 4 SofTT | | | | 1.12.43 | | |
| 99/44 | | AvBa.Co | | | | 30.4.44 | 99/44 | |
| | | 4 PoF 11 | | | | 6.5.44 | | |
| 125/44 | | 51 Base | | | | 17/6/44 | | |
| | | Aircrew SSR | | | | 11/6/44 | | |
| | | 51 Base | | | | | | |
| 177/44 | | 207.Sqdn. | | | | 14/9/44 | | |
| 100/44 | | missing | | | | 18/19/12/44 | | |
| 142/44 | | WCA D | | | | 19/12/44 | | |
| PEL 1883/173 | | Death Presumed | | | | 18/12/44 | | |
| | Killed | in Action | | | | 15.12.44 | | |

*Eric Hall's RAF service record.*

search engine, the Internet and a bit of common sense it's possible to put together a theoretical history of his service for further investigation. There are some excellent websites devoted to the RAF, though, as ever, some caution should always be exercised, especially with unofficial sites.

When looking at the service record squadrons are usually named as such, i.e. 207 Squadron, and RAF station names are usually in capital letters, though in this case there's no obvious station named. For other postings you'll need to use the search facility on TNA's website remembering that AIR 29 is the series that contains the record books for RAF Miscellaneous Units, including training centres, schools and depots. There are a few basic principles that might help – S is frequently School; A is often Air; AC Aircrew; R can be Radio or Reception; P is Personnel; Sq is Squadron. If you look at Appendix 4 you can get a good idea of the kinds of things letters represent to help you with your search. One thing to keep in mind is that the various record books referred to are not available online so a visit to TNA at Kew is necessary to look at them.

Searching AIR 29 under the number 2 and restricting the year range to 1943 provides 127 options, though many are easily discounted. Given that this is his first RAF posting it seems reasonable to assume that this is No. 2 Recruit Centre at Cardington, the records of which are in AIR 29/496. From here the record shows he was posted to the RAF Reserve which basically means he was sent home until required. It must have been decided that he was suitable for service in aircrew because on 20 September he was posted to 1 ACRC, which stands for Aircrew Reception Centre. Curiously, I can't trace a record book for the centre in the AIR records but searches of the Internet suggest that this may have been in London, at Lord's Cricket Ground.

From 1 ACRC he was posted to 21 ITW, which should be 21 Initial Training Wing – but again there doesn't appear to be a record book for this unit. It may be that this is a misspelling and should be 2 ITW, the clerk completing the form having written the I twice. 2 Initial Training Wing was based at Cambridge and the wing record book is in AIR 29/632. A search on the Internet at: http://www.rafweb.org/Stations/Stations, however, suggests that 21 Initial Training Wing may have been at RAF Bridlington for part of this time. This is obviously something that will require further investigation.

In December 1943 he was posted to No. 4 School of Technical Training at St Athan near Cardiff.

The school record book is in AIR 29/737. A Google search on '4 School of Technical Training' brings up a fascinating memoir of time at the school by a former RAF sergeant at: http://www.bbc.co.uk/ww2peopleswar/stories/69/a7798369.shtml. Eric Hall's service record shows a brief period of a week when he was posted to A V Roe & Co. in May 1944. A V Roe were the builders of the Avro Lancaster and the BBC memoir describes a similar posting to the AV Roe factory at Woodford near Stockport, and I suspect that Eric was sent to the same place and attended the same kinds of training and lectures described.

Following his time at the school Eric was posted to 51 Base and searching TNA's records using 'Base' and '51' in AIR 29 produces the record book for 'No. 51 R.A.F. Base, Morton Hall, later Swinderby, later No. 75 Base Swinderby'. This is in AIR 29/853. Searching the Internet looking for '51 R.A.F. Base, Morton Hall' reveals a fascinating website devoted to the RAF in Lincolnshire at: http://www.raf-lincolnshire.info, which confirms that RAF Morton Hall was Headquarters of 5 Group, Bomber Command in 1944 and that 207 Squadron was part of the Group. Since Eric Hall was posted to 207 Squadron this seems to be correct. At Morton Hall he spent three months at Aircrew School before going on to serve with 207 Bomber Squadron. The squadron record book covering Eric's period with 207 Squadron is in AIR 27/1236.

Using the record book it will be possible to find the aircraft and crew members that Eric flew with and the missions he flew. There will usually be a brief description of the raid, which may include mention of any air combats with German aircraft. Records of these combats are available online at TNA website in the DocumentsOnline section in the AIR 50 series. These reports can be searched by squadron, pilot and date and a quick look shows two reports from 23 September 1944 which may be of interest.

The official RAF website at: http://www.raf.mod.uk/organisation/207squadron.cfm gives a brief history of 207 Squadron, confirming that it flew Lancaster bombers and missions as far afield as Poland and Italy, though it has nothing specific to say about Eric's period with them.

The website of the Squadron Association at: http://www.207squadron.rafinfo.org.uk also has a brief history, which confirms '207 Squadron flew on 540 operations, by both day and night for the loss of 154 crews killed or missing, with at least another 9 aircraft lost on non-operational flights'.

The record concludes with Sergeant Hall's presumed death on 18 December 1944. The Debt of Honour website of the Commonwealth War Graves Commission at: http://www.cwgc.org/debt_of_honour.asp?menu allows one to search for details of casualties. Using Eric's surname and initials, year of death and the fact he was in the RAF, it reveals that his body was never recovered and that he is listed on the RAF's Runnymede Memorial to the Missing on Panel 230. It confirms his date of death as 18 December 1944 and that he was the son of George Alfred and Violet Ethel Maud Hall, of Upper Tooting, London. He was 19 years of age.

## Operations Record Books (ORBs)

Once you have used the service record to establish a chronology of places and squadrons served in you can turn to their Operations Records Books for more detailed information on what they did. They are the key documents for finding out what the RAF unit your relative was posted to was doing on a day-to-day basis.

ORBs, comprising both Summary of Events Forms (Form 540) and Detail of Work Carried Out Forms (Form 541), together with their appendices (usually operational orders, miscellaneous reports and telegraphed messages) are a record of daily events kept by all units of the RAF. If you are lucky an ORB will contain lists of names (for example, on duty, or on transfers of personnel elsewhere) and some contain photographs. The information recorded can vary, often depending on circumstances at the time the ORB was written – some squadron and station records from the Battle of Britain period are sketchy. Quite simply there was far too much going on for time to be spent on the luxury of writing up the ORB. There are also occasional gaps – 605 Squadron was overrun by the Japanese on Java in 1942 and their ORB for their period in the Far East must be presumed lost in the rout. During quiet periods, particularly for some of the smaller training or depot units, all you might get is a note 'nothing of interest to report'.

Though ORBs were kept at command, group and wing level (in AIR 24, AIR 25 and AIR 26 respectively) the ones most likely to be of interest in researching a relative are the ones for squadrons, stations and Miscellaneous Units (AIR 27, AIR 28 and AIR 29 respectively). Quite often you'll be able to refer to ORBs for both the squadron and the station it was based at.

ORBs usually list aircraft and, in the case of bomber or other large aircraft, the full crew, with some note of what each man was doing. For bomber raids there is usually a brief description of the part each aircraft played telling you what they saw, where they dropped their bombs, detailing any damage and giving a brief summary of any combats. To get a larger picture of events, particularly for large bomber raids or some of the fiercer days of fighting during the Battle of Britain, it is frequently worth looking up the ORBs for the wings or groups that a squadron was part of.

When searching for group ORBs via TNA website search engine you'll need to be aware that the name of the group frequently reflected its role, so that 1 Group cannot be found by a simple search on that term. No. 1 Group is actually referred to as NO. 1 (BOMBER) GROUP and its ORBs can be traced using this reference. If you're not sure of the exact title but have the number of the group the good news is that until 1946 the records are in numerical order so you can browse through until you find the ones you want.

## Log Books

Even without a service record, if you have a relative's Flying Log Book you can tell an enormous amount about their career. Everyone who flew had a log book, not just pilots and navigators, and not just RAF servicemen – the Army Air Corps and the Fleet Air Arm used them too and recorded similar information in them.

Log books will tell you which RAF stations (or Army bases or ships) a man was attached to; which squadon(s) he served with; the aircraft he flew (both the type of aircraft and its individual number), who the pilot was, the nature of the flight (training, air experience, testing, operational), where it was to, the role played by the log book's owner (pilot, navigator, gunner, bomb aimer) and the duration of the flight. You can build up a very clear picture of a man's career both from the information in the log book and from following up the leads it provides.

## Case Study – Flight Sergeant R W Horton's Log Book

Flight Sergeant R W Horton flew as a navigator with 295 Squadron and 46 (Uganda) Squadron on Stirling bombers used for the towing of gliders and transport. He took part in Operation Tonga, the glider drop that immediately preceded the D-Day landings and in Operation Market, the landing of troops near Arnhem, as well as in smaller drops into France.

The back of Sergeant Horton's log book includes a section for any Proficiency Assessments, in which he has noted all the stations he visited and served on as aircrew – but he also listed all the stations served on, including his initial postings, so that his early career can be reconstructed. Though we don't know when he was called up, his first posting was to the London Aircrew Reception Centre then to No. 5 Wing (Initial Training Wing) at Torquay, where he would have been given basic training and technical assessments. He must have shown some aptitude as a navigator because he was then posted to No. 1 Elementary Air Navigation School, first at Eastbourne and later at Bridgnorth. Having done his ground-based training he was posted to an Air Familiarisation Unit.

Sergeant Horton's log book, in terms of actual flying, opens with his very first air experience flights at Number 10 (AFU) at Dumfries. At the AFU (Air Familiarisation Unit), after a couple of flights just to get used to aircraft, he took part in flights training the crew in navigational equipment and techniques, air photography and undertook a series of long-distance navigational training flights, mainly over the Irish Sea. He was then posted, in May 1943, to No. 30 Operational Training Unit at Hixton, with their flying being done at RAF Seighford. It's clear from the log book that here the aircrew were being trained, as the name suggest, for operational flying – the log records flights that included high-level bombing, air-to-air firing, formation flying and, on 1 July 1943, a final operational flight to Nantes.

Sergeant Horton was posted to 295 Squadron, based at Hurn in Dorset, at the end of July 1943. 295 were dedicated to working with the Army's Airborne Forces, paratroops and glider borne infantry. Training was intense, with practice flights involving the dropping of dummy troops, live troops, formation flying and the towing and dropping of gliders.

There are several operational flights that feature in the log book which appear unusual. On 4 March 1944 there's a flight noted as 'Operations – BUTLER 16 – France'; on 11 April 'Operations France – Phono 7'; on 7 August 'Operations – IAN 7 – France'; on 25 August 'Operations – DONKEYMAN 73 – France'; on 31 August 'Operations – DITCHER 40 – France'; on 5 September 'Operations – BOB 337 – France'; on 10 September 'Operations – PERCY 34 –

| Date | Hour | Aircraft Type and No. | Pilot | Duty | Remarks (including results of bombing, gunnery, exercises, etc.) | Flying Times Day | Flying Times Night |
|---|---|---|---|---|---|---|---|
| 12/5/44 | 21.30 | ALBEMARLE 1461 | F/LT WOOD | NAVIGATOR | EXERCISE FREE II - XC TOW | | 1.25 |
| 15/5/44 | 14.20 | 1461 | F/LT WOOD | NAVIGATOR | EXERCISE 'SALUTE' - REBECCA RUN UP | 1.20 | |
| 16/5/44 | 10.40 | 1461 | F/LT WOOD | NAVIGATOR | LOCAL TOW | .45 | |
| 20/5/44 | 1810 | 1777 | F/LT WOOD | NAVIGATOR | BASE - NETHERAVON | .20 | |
| 20/5/44 | 1900 | 1777 | F/LT WOOD | NAVIGATOR | NETHERAVON - BASE WITH GLIDER | .30 | |
| 22/5/44 | 10.30 | 1184 OXFORD | F/LT WOOD | NAVIGATOR | LOCAL TOW | .55 | |
| 23/5/44 | 10.00 | R5890 | P/O PEEL | INSTRUCTION | G - TRAINING | .45 | |
| | | | | | TOTAL FLYING FOR MAY | 7.30 | 13.25 |
| | | | | | PREVIOUS TOTAL | 309.05 | 122.25 |
| | | | | | GRAND TOTAL | 316.35 | 137.50 |
| | | | | CERTIFIED CORRECT [signature] F/Lt S/LDR | | | |
| | | | | O.C B'FLIGHT 295 | | | |
| 1/6/44 | 1450 | 1461 | F/LT WOOD | NAVIGATOR | AIR TEST | .25 | |
| 3/6/44 | 1530 | 1461 | F/LT WOOD | NAVIGATOR | AIR TEST | .30 | |
| 5/6/44 | 0930 | 1461 | F/LT WOOD | NAVIGATOR | AIR TEST | .50 | |
| 6/6/44 | 0135 | 1461 | F/LT WOOD | NAVIGATOR | OPERATION TONGA - HEAVY TOW-NORMANDY | | 3.30 |
| 10/6/44 | 0945 | 1461 | F/LT WOOD | NAVIGATOR | AIR TEST | .30 | |
| 13/6/44 | 1625 | 1461 | F/LT WOOD | NAVIGATOR | AIR TEST | .30 | |
| | | | | | TOTAL TIME ... | 319.20 | 141.20 |

*Part of Flight Sergeant Horton's log book showing his participation in Operation Tonga – the glider drop for D-Day.*

France'; on 2 October 'Operations – MESSENGER 41 – France'; and finally on 24 November 'Operations – THRUSH RED 3 – Norway – unsuccessful – landed Lossiemouth'. It's unlikely that Horton knew very much at all about these operations, which were presumably to drop either agents or supplies into France for the Special Operations Executive (SOE) or the Secret Intelligence Service (SIS).

On 17 September 1944 Horton flew as navigator in Stirling LK120, with Flying Officer Taylor as pilot, on an operational flight – 'Market – Heavy Tow – Holland'. This was the first airborne drop to try and capture and hold the Rhine bridge at Arnhem and presumably they were towing one of the gliders. Just two days later they were back over Holland as part of Market III. The log book gives no more details of their part in the action.

In July 1944 the log book records a brief posting to No. 1665 Heavy Conversion Unit at Tilstock, where he trained, with his usual pilot, Flight Lieutenant Wood, in flying the Stirling bomber.

Sergeant Horton was posted to No. 46 (Uganda) Squadron on 29 January 1945. The squadron were reforming as a transport squadron, equipped with Stirling bombers modified to carry troops. In April 1945 Horton undertook a series of long-distance flights, starting from RAF Stoney Cross and carrying troops to Mauripur in India via North Africa, Italy and the Middle East. Other long-distance transport flights involved trips to Gibraltar, Egypt and Malta.

His final flight (as a passenger) was in a Dakota on 8 April 1946. Presumably he received his discharge from the RAF shortly afterwards.

The ORB for 30 OUT is in Air 29 series (Operational Record Books, Miscellaneous Units) in AIR 29/672.

The squadron ORB for 295 Squadron, covering its whole wartime service, 1942 to 1946, is in AIR 27/1644.

The ORB for 1665 Heavy Conversion Unit is in AIR 29/614.

The ORB's for 46 (Uganda) Squadron covering 1945–6 are in AIR 27/461 and AIR 27/2417/1.

There are reports on the RAF part of Operation Tonga in AIR 37/553 (Airborne plan: Operation 'Tonga'); AIR 37/286 (No. 38 GROUP (38 WING): Operation 'Overlord', Operation 'Tonga'); and AIR 37/976 (No. 38 GROUP (38 WING): Operation order No. 501: Operation 'Tonga').

There are a dozen easily identifiable files on the RAF contribution to the Arnhem operations at TNA. Among those most likely to be of interest to anyone researching Sergeant Horton are a series of files in AIR 37 covering the operations of 38 Group during the battle. These are AIR 37/259, AIR 37/260, AIR 37/261 and AIR 37/1217. Other files (try using TNA's search engine using the search term 'Market' in the AIR series for 1944) cover Fighter Command's contribution and air operations as a whole.

## A Useful Aid – the RAF Confidential List

During the Second World War the *RAF List* was in two parts. The first contained officers, with their ranks and seniority, but gave no information about their postings. The second part, which was necessary for administrative purposes, detailed stations, the units based at them, the officers attached to them for administrative and command purposes and their postal addresses. This list was published and circulated on a very strictly controlled basis. If you have a Second World War RAF service record it will usually list stations or units (often simply by number and/or initials) and the RAF Confidential List is an ideal way of tracking down what the unit was, and where it was based. Appendix 4 gives a list of many of the abbreviations used by the RAF and in conjunction with the Confidential Lists (held between AIR 10/3814 ('The Air Ministry Confidential Air Force List April–May 1939') and AIR 10/5421('The Air Ministry Confidential Air Force List July–December 1953') you should be able to identify which units they served in and where they were.

The List is divided into commands and then groups, and each group contains a list of the squadrons and units that were part of it. For each group, in addition to the squadrons and flights that it comprises, there are lists of the various Air Staff, Administrative and Service officers who are employed.

Home Units (units based in Britain) are listed geographically so that, for example, RAF Belfast comprises the RAF Station HQ; HQ RAF Northern

Ireland; HQ No. 82 Group; No. 968 Squadron; Queens University Air Squadron; No. 11 RAF Embarkation Unit; Northern Ireland Recruiting HQ; the RAF Movement Control Officer; No. 2 Heavy Mobile W/T Section; the Superintending Engineer, No. 16 Works Area; the Section Officer AMWD and No. 8 Ferry Pilots Pool. There are details of each postal address, telegraphic address and telephone numbers and details of local railway stations.

Overseas Units are also listed geographically, both by commands and by type of unit so that, for example, Helwan (Egypt) houses the Station HQ; Code and Cypher School; No. 1411 Flight (Met); Film Production Unit; No. 2 P R Unit, British Airways Repair Unit; Command Medical Board; No. 1 Australian Air Ambulance Unit and No. 22 Sector Operations Room. Various medical units are listed, including the RAF Hospitals, Convalescent Depots, WAAF Convalescent Depots, the Hospital Base Accounts Office and Medical Stores Depot. The Miscellaneous Units are listed alphabetically, starting with the Aeroplane Armament Experimental Establishment at Boscombe Down and the Airborne Forces Experimental Establishment at Ringway, and include various Flying Boat Repair Stations, Mobile Torpedo Bases, Packed Aircraft Transit Pools, Photographic Reconnaissance Units and the Inspectorate of Recruiting.

## Combat Reports

The RAF, as a technical service, always tried to collect information on aircraft performance and to analyse it to assist with development. It also collected information on combats so enemy tactics could be scrutinised and new counter tactics devised. All pilots engaged in a combat (not just fighter pilots) were interviewed by the Squadron Intelligence Officer very soon after landing and asked to talk through the fight. This material is collected in TNA's AIR 50 series. Initial reports were sparse but later ones were written on pre-printed forms so that information collected was standardised.

A typical report from Warrant Officer Dean with 135 Squadron records:

I opened fire on port a/c from 300 yards dead astern holding the burst as the range closed. Enemy a/c banked slowly to port and I continued to fire using deflection to a range of 50 yards. Total length of burst estimated at 8 seconds. E/A commenced to pour out thick black smoke from the motor which enveloped the fuselage and half the main-planes as it rolled over and went down.

The report gives many other details of the action, including the loss of a Hurricane. If your relative flew in combat missions their reports should be in AIR 50, but please note that not all have survived.

Combat Reports are now available online at TNA's website in their DocumentsOnline section. They can be searched under individual name or by squadron. Some typical reports from some of the squadrons that took part in the Battle of Britain can be found in:

| | |
|---|---|
| Air 50/21 | '54 Squadron, Combat Reports, February 1940 to November 1941' |
| Air 50/25 | '65 (East India) Squadron, Combat Reports, May 1940 to April 1945' |
| Air 50/32 | '74 Squadron, Combat Reports, November 1939 to November 1945' |
| Air 50/18 | '41 Squadron, Combat Reports, October 1939 to May 1945' |
| Air 50/105 | '266 (Rhodesia) Squadron, Combat Reports, June 1940 to April 1945' |
| Air 50/164 | '600 Squadron, Combat Reports, May 1940 to April 1945' |
| Air 50/104 | '264 Squadron, Combat Reports, May 1940 to March 1945' |
| Air 50/167 | '603 Squadron, Combat Reports, October 1939 to February 1942' |

## The RAF Regiment

The RAF Regiment was formed in 1942 in response to problems the RAF had encountered since the beginning of the war in protecting their airfields. Heavy losses had been suffered in France in 1940 when retreating units had been overrun. During the Battle of Britain it was felt there was insufficient anti-aircraft defence and in Crete in 1941 the principal RAF base at Malame was overrun by German paratroops with little defence being offered.

The new RAF Regiment was composed of Anti-Aircraft Flights and Field Squadrons, but all members of the Regiment were initially trained as infantrymen.

The Regiment absorbed the RAF Armoured Car Units that had served in Iraq since 1921.

AIR 29/50 includes the ORB for the No. 1 Armoured Car Company which took part in the dramatic defence of RAF Habbaniya in 1941 when it was besieged by Iraqi forces. The ORB notes, at 0500 hrs on 30 April 1941: 'Iraqi Forces invested Cantonment and issued ultimatum to cease flying or shelling would commence. The ultimatum was rejected. The Company stood by at instant notice.' There was fierce fighting as the Iraqi's attempted to capture the base and on 2 May the ORB says:

No. 3 Section made a Sortie with a view to attacking six enemy armoured cars in position on the south side of the aerodrome. Five attacks were made and fire was opened at approximately 400 yards range, with armour piercing machine gun bullets, scoring hits on the enemy but not disabling any of them. All our vehicles returned safely. There were no casualties but several punctures were caused by enemy fire.

ORBs for the RAF Regiment are in AIR 29: AIR 29/883, for example, covers No. 4010 Anti-Aircraft Flight at RAF Skitten, near Wick in Scotland. Searching for individual units can be slightly complicated – some units are indexed under 'Regiment', others under 'Regt' or under 'Field Squadron'.

## Women in the RAF

Women served in the RAF in growing numbers throughout the war in both the Women's Auxiliary Air Force (WAAF) and Princess Mary's Royal Air Force Nursing Service. WAAF and nurses' service records are held by the MOD. To gain information write to: RAF Disclosures Section, Room 221b, Trenchard Hall, RAF Cranwell, Sleaford, Lincolnshire, NG34 8HB; tel: 01400 261201, ext 6711, ext 8161/8159 (officers), ext 8163/8168/8170 (other ranks), using the same forms from the Veterans Agency website at: http://www.veterans-uk.info. You can trace a servicewoman's career using the same methods as for a serviceman.

### RAF Nurses

The Royal Air Force Nursing Service was founded on 1 June 1918 and established as a permanent part of the RAF by Royal Charter in January 1921. Princess Mary became Royal Patron in June that year and the service was renamed Princess Mary's Royal Air Force Nursing Service. The first RAF nurses went to serve in Iraq in 1922. During the Second World War RAF nurses served in every theatre. By 1943 there were thirty-one RAF Hospitals and seventy-one Station Sick Quarters.

Papers relating to RAF Medical Services during the Second World War are in TNA's AIR 49 Series. Though these are usually compiled on a command or district level they often contain reports from individual RAF medical units. The ORBs for the hospitals and other medical units are in AIR 29.

An excellent website for the service is at: http://www.pmrafns.org/index.htm which gives a brief history of the service, along with details of the current service and careers for RAF nurses.

### The Women's Auxiliary Air Force

The Women's Auxiliary Air Force was formed on 28 June 1939. Though in the First World War most women had been given domestic and clerking jobs, it was always intended that the WAAF would work in such front-line posts as radar operators and in sector control. As the war continued WAAF servicewomen took up posts in meteorology, transport, telephony and telegraphy, codes and ciphers, Intelligence, Security and Operation Rooms.

There are numerous files on women's service in the Air Force in the AIR 2 series detailing pay, conditions and some of the perceived problems of having women serving alongside men. On the whole WAAFs were considered to have done a splendid job and in 1949 the WAAF was reformed as the Women's Royal Air Force and was amalgamated with the RAF in 1994.

Service records for WAAFs and WRAFs are still held by the Ministry of Defence so to access them you'll need to write to RAF Cranwell. The service record will tell you the units your relative was posted to and you can search for unit records in the relevant AIR series. Group and wing records are again in AIR 25 and AIR 26 and AIR 27, AIR 28 and AIR 29 Squadrons, Stations and Miscellaneous Units respectively. Foreign Command records are in AIR 24.

There is an excellent website devoted to the WAAF at: http:// www.waafassociation.org.uk.

### *The Air Transport Auxiliary*

This was a civilian organisation run by BOAC, delivering aircraft from factories to RAF stations. Though the vast majority of its pilots were men it did employ some women pilots, as well as administrative staff. By the end of the war over 1,150 men and 600 women had served in the ATA. Service records (including administrative, catering and other staff) are at the RAF Museum, Hendon (see section below), with a seventy-five-year embargo if you're not next of kin. You'll have to prove that you're next of kin, or provide their authority (or the authority of the person themselves), to receive a copy.

The AVIA series at TNA contains records of the ATA, particularly in AVIA 27, with additional material in AIR 15.

An excellent site devoted to the ATA can be found at: http:// www.airtransportaux.com, with sections on its history, various articles and photographs.

## Other Useful RAF Records and Sources

### *Courts Martial*

Courts Martial are the military (including the RAF) courts for trying servicemen (and some civilians abroad) for crimes committed while under military jurisdiction. The service record will give you certain basic information if your relative was tried in a military court. The section 'Time Forefeited', i.e. time in the service that does not count towards a pension, will tell you if they lost time because of a Court Martial sentence and will give you the date of the trial. This is all you need to get started. Though most Court Martial papers are lost or still retained, there are registers available which will give you basic details.

The registers detailing RAF Court Martial charges give the name and rank of each prisoner, place of trial, nature of the charge and sentence in AIR 21 series. Charges listed are: desertion, absence, striking or violence, insubordination or disobedience, leaving post, drunkenness, theft, fraud, cheque fraud, indecency, resisting escort, escaping confinement, scandalous conduct, self-inflicted wound, miscellaneous. Miscellaneous charges include specific offences against King's Regulations – the number quoted in the column refers to the specific regulation breached. AIR 10/2279 is a copy of the King's Regulations and Air Council Instructions for the Royal Air Force that should clarify the nature of the offence.

In addition to the basic charges you may find additional letters in the column that will help flesh out the details of the alleged offence. These are:

| | |
|---|---|
| ABH | Actual Bodily Harm |
| CA | Common Assault |
| WI | Wounding with Intent |
| W | Wounding |
| SB&L | Shop Breaking & Larceny |
| HB&L | House Breaking & Larceny |
| B&E | Breaking & Entering |
| WD | Wilful Damage |
| MFD | Making False Document |
| POSB | Post Office Savings Book |
| Forgery | Forgery |
| R (in theft column) | Receiving |
| FP | False Pretences |

Surviving papers on individual trials are in AIR 18 and many indexed references include names of individuals so a search on the TNA website is worth a go. Unfortunately, some charges are indexed by one name and then 'and others' so you may need more information from a service record to help you trace further information. Some papers remain closed but there's nothing to stop you attempting to have them opened using a Freedom of Information Act application. If the file is closed the TNA catalogue allows you to make an application online.

Typical documents in the AIR 18 files include: summaries of evidence, witness statements to the court, lists of exhibits, descriptions of the exhibits, service-record summaries, lists of witnesses, statements given to the Police, transcripts of the trial, records of proceedings naming the members of the Court Martial and defending and prosecuting counsels, and legal notes on the proceedings by the Advocate General.

**Please bear in mind that many participants in Courts Martial in AIR 18 are likely to still be alive and take care in using the information you may find in the records.**

AIR 43 records comprise the Judge Advocate General's Office: Royal Air Force Courts Martial Charge Books covering 1918 to 1948. These consist of the opinions of the Judge Advocate General's Department on evidence to be used in various cases, on the nature of the charges to be pressed and the procedure. Only occasionally is a verdict recorded. The files are chronological so if you know from an individual's service record that a Court Martial was held you can check the relevant AIR 43 file to see if any papers are there. The files aren't indexed but do appear to be scrupulously in date order so it shouldn't take long. For many cases, apart from the record in AIR 21 the AIR 43 papers will be the only official papers remaining.

AIR 71 records are administrative papers (Out letters) relating to Courts Martial and are bound chronologically so if you know the date of the trial you can locate any relevant documents.

## Gallantry and Distinguished Service Awards

Recommendations for Second World War awards are in the AIR 2 series and submission papers to the King are in AIR 30. Not only are there recommendations for serving personnel but also for civilians involved in the air services or events involving aircraft (such as accidents and crashes). There are awards for instructors, bomb-disposal personnel, test pilots and to prisoners of war.

To flying personnel awards fell into two categories, immediate awards (for individual acts of bravery) and non-immediate (for extended periods such as bomber tours of operation). The recommendations are grouped by command (Bomber, Fighter, Coastal, Middle East etc.) and chronologically. Some typical examples for Bomber Command include:

AIR 2/4072 'Recommendations for awards to R.A.F. personnel: Bomber Command operations 1939–1940'
AIR 2/4094 'Immediate awards to R.A.F. personnel: Bomber Command operations 1939–1940'
AIR 2/6085 'Bomber Command Non-immediate awards 1940–1941'
AIR 2/8748 'Non-immediate awards: Bomber Command 1945–1946'
AIR 2/9447 'Immediate awards: Bomber Command 1940 July–Aug'

Fighter Command awards covering the Battle of Britain are in:

AIR 2/4086 'Recommendations for Honours and Awards (non-immediate): Fighter Command operations'
AIR 2/4095 'Immediate awards to R.A.F. personnel: Fighter Command operations'
AIR 2/8351 'Non-immediate awards: Fighter Command, Sept. 1940'
AIR 2/9468 'Non-immediate awards: Fighter Command 1940 Aug–Sept'

Immediate awards tend to be recommended across the RAF as a whole so if you don't know why an award was made (and many, including the Distinguished Service Order and the Distinguished Flying Cross could be awarded for both individual acts of gallantry and for long periods of bravery) you may need to check several files, even if you know the date of gazette. There are thirteen files of recommendations for 1943 alone.

Awards for ground gallantry include awards to soldiers who assisted the RAF, as well as to RAF regiment soldiers and to airmen serving at aerodromes.

AIR 2 also includes recommendations to civilians and other serviceman recommended by the Air Ministry for awards for assisting the RAF including, on one occasion, a schoolboy recommended for kicking through a glass door to rescue a baby trapped by a crashed aircraft. He received a commendation, as well as two days off school with lacerated feet!

A professional researcher, Paul Baillie, has indexed all the recommendations within AIR 2. He can be contacted via email at: paulbaillie@tiscali.co.uk. For a very reasonable fee he can check his index and provide you with a copy of any surviving recommendation.

## Casualties and Prisoners of War

The Memorial to the Missing of the Royal Air Force is an impressive monument built overlooking Runnymede, near Egham and is always worth a visit, if only to appreciate the sheer numbers of men (and a very few women of the Air Transport Auxiliary) who were lost and have no known grave. The RAF's own church at St Clement Danes on the Strand, a beautiful building with the badges of RAF squadrons inlaid into the floor, contains the RAF Roll of Honour. Individual squadrons and stations may also have Rolls of Honour and there are Rolls of Honour for various Bomber Command Groups in York, Ely and Lincoln cathedrals, reflecting the vital importance of the east-coast areas as bases for the bomber campaign against Germany.

RAF prisoners of war completed MI9 questionnaires at the end of the war and their forms are held with those of their fellow prisoners in WO 344 series and can be quite illuminating about the circumstances of their capture and subsequent imprisonment. There are rolls of RAF prisoners in AIR 20/2336. RAF prisoners of war were held by their German equivalent, the Luftwaffe and you can identify their camps because they were all called Stalag Luft followed by a number. There are numerous reports on these camps, their prisoners and conditions in the AIR 40 records between AIR 40/263 ('Stalag Luft I, Barth, Germany: nominal roll, short report by Wg. Cdr. F.M. Hilton and correspondence') and AIR 40/279 ('Stalag Luft 1, Barth, Germany: miscellaneous documents; Gp. Capt. C.T. Weir's file (Senior British Officer)'). If you know the name of a relative's POW camp then a search on TNA catalogue should produce a variety of reports.

## The RAF Museum

The RAF Museum at Hendon (RAF Museum London, Grahame Park Way, London, NW9 5LL) not only holds an extensive collection of RAF aircraft throughout its history, but an extensive archive which may be of use to family and local historians. You can download documents about researching RAF ancestors and details of the kinds of information they hold from their website at: http://www.rafmuseum.org.uk. The site also provides useful links to various RAF association websites through which you may be able to trace old comrades of a relative.

The Museum archive holds microfilm copies of Accident Record Cards giving details of aircraft accidents. These are only indexed by type and date so if seeking information on a specific crash you'll have to already know quite a lot about it. During the Second World War Bomber Command was keen to analyse information on aircraft losses and kept cards giving details of crew names, their fate, route taken and bomb load. Occasionally details such as specific aircraft modifications are included.

From the years 1938 to 1947 there are the 'Particulars of Non Effective Account' records, which give details of what happened to the effects and final pay of men killed (or committed as insane). There are usually some details of the casualty and next of kin.

The archive holds an extensive collection of aircrew log books covering the whole history of the RFC and RAF, mostly donated by ex-servicemen or their families.

There is much donated material in the form of photograph albums, diaries and personal papers. These range from Lord Trenchard's papers and letters to material provided by ordinary airmen. I particularly enjoyed the diary of an aircraftsman from the 1920s who served in India which described his technical exams, an aircraft crash and leave in an RAF bungalow.

The library collection holds over 13,000 books, 34,000 periodical volumes (including *Flight, Popular Flying* and *Aeroplane* magazines), over 50,000 manuals, 8,500 air diagrams and 6,000 maps.

The Museum can be contacted through their website at: http://www.rafmuseum.org.uk or via email at: london@rafmuseum.org or by telephone on 02082 052266 (General Information).

The official website of the RAF at: http://www.raf.mod.uk has a useful history section which has a great deal of formation on squadrons, stations and famous RAF battles such as the Battle of Britain and the Bomber Command campaign against Germany.

*Chapter 6*

# THE MERCHANT NAVY

The Merchant Navy was the lifeline that kept the country supplied with food, fuel, raw material and equipment throughout the war, in the face of an intense campaign by German submarines, aircraft and surface raiders. Casualties among men and shipping were enormous. Life expectancy among merchant seamen in 1942 and 1943, before the U-boat menace was defeated, was low, with casualties as high as one man in three.

The heaviest losses were suffered in the Atlantic, but convoys making their way to Russia around the North Cape and those supplying Malta in the Mediterranean were also particularly vulnerable to attack. In all, 4,786 merchant ships were lost during the war with a total of 32,000 lives. More than a quarter of this total was lost in home waters.

The government took control of the merchant marine at the start of the Second World War because its role was so important. In 1941 they introduced a new Central Register of Seamen and all merchant sailors who had been to sea in the previous five years were required to register. For the first time seamen got paid when not actually at sea as they were now considered available for a voyage at any time.

Unlike their contemporaries in the armed forces, there is much available online about the Merchant Seamen (and women) and the ships in which they served.

## Merchant Navy Medal Records

Available online, at TNA's DocumentsOnline in series BT 395, are the records of Second World War medals claimed and issued to Merchant Seamen (or their family – my grandmother claimed her late father's medal in 1951) from 1946 to 2002. Medals were not automatically issued but had to be claimed. Following the war, medal papers were raised including details of a seaman's service. These were sent to ports for the veteran to sign, confirming the accuracy of the information, and were then returned to the Registrar General of Shipping and Seamen in Cardiff.

Each entry gives details of the seaman's name and the medals, ribbons and clasps issued, together with a reference to the medal-papers file, held at the Registry of Shipping and Seamen. Usually, the sailor's discharge book number and date and place of birth are also listed.

*Interpreting the Medal Record*

Merchant Seamen were eligible for eight of the Second World War campaign medals:

**The War Medal** – for which they'd have had to have served a minimum of twenty-eight days at sea.

**The 1939–45 Star** – for six months' service at sea, including one voyage in an operational area.

**Atlantic Star** – for service in North Russian waters, home waters and North and South Atlantics after having already qualified for the 1939–45 medal.

**Africa Star** – for service in the Mediterranean and off the coast of Morocco between 10 June 1940–12 May 1943.

**Pacific Star** – for service in Pacific or Indian Oceans and South China Sea after 8 December 1941 after having already qualified for the 1939–45 medal.

**Burma Star** – for service in the Bay of Bengal after 11 December 1941 after having already qualified for the 1939–45 medal.

**France and Germany Star (1944–5)** – for service in direct support of land operations in France, Belgium, Holland and Germany and in the North Sea.

**Italy Star** – for service in the Mediterranean and Aegean, off Corsica, Greece and Yugoslavia between 11 June 1943–8 May 1945 after having already qualified for the 1939–45 medal.

The Merchant Navy Association Archive holds complete records of all Merchant Seamen killed during wartime (full name, rating, ship, date, age and home town). It also holds records of their ships, how they were lost (cause of loss, U-boat details, time and place of attack, voyage and cargo, references to official records at TNA), details of all decorations awarded to Merchant Seamen for the Second World War and the 'keys' to locating the service cards of Merchant Seamen 1918–41 at TNA.

# Merchant Navy Service Records

*Officers*

The best source of information on careers of Merchant Navy Ship's Masters (Captains) are the Lloyds Captains' Registers, compiled by Lloyds Insurance and available on microfilm at TNA. These are arranged alphabetically and contain, for each Ship's Master (unofficially known as the Captain), their name, date and place of birth; date, number and place of issue of their master's certificate; details of any special qualifications; names and numbers of each ship commanded, date of engagement and discharge; destination of voyages and casualties; details of war service, including awards.

The original registers are held at the Guildhall Library, Aldermanbury, London, EC2P 2EJ. There are other microfilmed copies of the registers at the

National Maritime Museum at Greenwich. There's a guide to using the micro-filmed registers at the National Maritime Museum at: http://www.nmm .ac.uk/researchers/library/research-guides/lloyds/lloyds-captains-registers.

Service records for junior officers (Ship's Mates, Engineers and Fishing Officers) comprise their Certificates of Competency, held on microfiche at TNA in their BT 352 series and made up of card indexes which record the name, date of birth, place of birth, certificate number, grade, date of passing and port of examination for each certificate gained.

## Seamen

The services of Merchant Seamen were recorded on a Central Register by the Board of Trade and two of the registers cover the Second World War. The first (The Fourth Register of Seamen) covers the period 1918–41, the second (The Fifth Register) is from 1941 onwards (though it includes details of men who'd been to sea in the previous five years).

The Fourth Register is available on microfiche in TNA's Open Reading Room and consists of four sets of cards held in four separate record series. BT 350 and BT 349 consist of the Central Index Cards for seamen. In BT 350 each card typically gives the following information: discharge A number; certificate of company number; name of seaman; year and place of birth; rank or rating; name and official number of ship and date of engagement of service. In BT 349 the cards typically give the same information but in addition their discharge A number; rating; RV2 number (origin unknown); certificate grade and number; PR number (origin unknown); health-insurance number; unemployment-insurance number and a physical description: height, colour of eyes and hair, complexion, distinguishing marks. The reverse of the card has the seaman's signature and the date of issue.

There are two additional sets of cards on microfiche: BT 348 cards show the ships a seaman served on, usually in the form of the ship's Registry number; BT 364 cards appear to be a compilation of information from other cards – usually for men who also appear in The Fifth Register. Both BT 348 and BT 364 are arranged numerically so you'll need to find this from the BT 349 and BT 350 cards, which are arranged alphabetically.

The Fifth Register records on a standard form (CRS 10) the service of individual Merchant Seamen and lists the ships on which they served with relevant dates. The CRS 10s give personal details of each seaman including, name, age, rank, rating/grade and qualifications. They provide details of ships served on, the names of ships and their official numbers, the dates of engagement and discharge and rank served. This information about service was extracted from ship's logs and crew agreements lodged by ship owners. The information contained in the register is used to verify entitlement to wartime service medals.

The Fifth Register was maintained in a number of parts or sub-series as follows:

Part One: covering mainly Europeans and mainly the period from 1941 to approximately 1946, although some late 1940s and 1950s records can also be found.

Part Two: covering mainly Europeans and mainly the period from 1946–72, although some records covering the Second World War period can also be found.

Part Three: Asiatic seamen, mostly from the Indian sub-continent, from 1942–65.

Part Four: Asiatic seamen, mostly from the Indian sub-continent, from 1966–72.

Part Five: Indian, Chinese and foreign national seamen, unnumbered series (as service was only of brief duration a discharge book/seamen's number were not allocated), mainly from 1941–72, although the records of Chinese seaman cover the period 1945–72.

Part Six: prisoners of war and internees; Europeans, Lascars (Indians), Adenese, Goanese and Chinese, from 1940–5.

Part Seven: records of those men who served on merchant vessels requisitioned for war services.

Part Eight: records of the deaths of Merchant Seamen recorded for pension purposes for the Ministry of Pensions, from 1944–51.

As well as providing some very basic information about the subject (date and place of birth, rank or rating and qualifications) the record cards in BT 382 will list all the ships that your relative served on in chronological order and, using these, you can find and download the relevant Merchant Shipping Movement Card(s) for each ship from TNA's BT 389 series. Each card records the name of the ship, any previous name it had, its size (tonnage), to whom it was registered, the ship's destination, date of arrival and sometimes ports of call. They also record any cargo carried on board. Importantly, the cards also show if the ship was torpedoed, mined, damaged or sunk. They do not contain details of any passengers or crew and are concerned only with details of the ship.

There's a very useful list of the abbreviations for service cards in a TNA research guide available online at: http://www.nationalarchives.gov.uk/records/research-guides/merchant-seamen-RGSS-register-abbreviations.htm.

## Case Study – My Merchant Navy Ancestors

I've always known that my great-grandfather Fred Lambert died in the Second World War – I remember going to see him on the Tower Hill Memorial as a small child. He has cards in The Fourth Register of Seamen which give details (by number) of the ships he served on during the 1920s and 1930s. I'm not aware of any photographs of Fred so it's useful to have a brief physical

*Frederick Lambert's Merchant Navy card noting him as believed drowned.*

description of him which says that he was 5ft 3in tall, had brown eyes, brown hair, a dark complexion and had the name 'Lizzie' (his wife) tattooed on both arms. There is a scrawled note on his main card which says 'Supposed drowned 31/4/40 on *Creofield*'. The Commonwealth War Graves Commission's Debt of Honour website records his death, confirming that he died on 31 January 1940 on the *Creofield* and gives the following personal information: 'Son of Frederick William and Caroline Lambert; husband of Mary Elizabeth Lambert, of North Shields, Northumberland'. He is commemorated on Panel 33 of the Tower Hill Memorial.

There are two cards for the *Creofield* in BT 389 which gives basic details of the vessel. It says that she was a tanker of 838 gross tonnage owned by Hunting & Son Ltd. Her voyages in British coastal waters and the North Sea throughout 1939 are recorded. On 28 January 1940 she left London for the Tees and was sighted off Southend on 31 January when she is noted as 'Overdue – Presumed lost. Lost by Kings Enemy Risks on or about 1/2/40. Sunk by enemy action, cause unknown, in North Sea 1/240.' Originally presumed to have struck a mine, it now appears she was sunk by German submarine *U-59* commanded by Kapitanleutnant Harald Jurst. The excellent website at: http://www.uboat.net/index.html says: 'At 06.24 hours on 2 Feb, 1940, the unescorted *Creofield* (Master Charles Fred Carlin) was hit amidships by one G7a torpedo from *U-59*, exploded and sank east of Lowestoft. The master and 15 crew members were lost.' Other sources say that a total of seventeen men were lost and my father eventually tracked down the Hunting

*My great-grandfather, Fred Lambert, commemorated on the Tower Hill Memorial.*

& Son Ltd war memorial which categorically names seventeen crewmen, including my great-grandfather.

One advantage of records going online (and there are many disadvantages) is that if they're indexed properly a search can produce some surprising results. One such is the result of my idly searching on the name Tomaselli on the TNA DocumentsOnline section of their website. I knew that there was a First World War soldier (no relation) in their First World War medal cards and vaguely wondered if there was anyone else. To my surprise there was a Merchant Seaman's medal listing for one 'Frank Tomaselli Cuthbert, Discharge number R194516, date of birth 29 May 1924'. I realised that this must have been one of my father's cousins – my great-grandfather Philippo Tomaselli married a widow with several children already, and I knew that two of her daughters had married into the Lambert family – they married two brothers. Having checked his seaman's cards it became clear that poor Frank had been killed during the war too, his card saying 'Supposed drowned 7/9/40 ex *Neptunian*'. The Commonwealth War Graves Commission's Debt of Honour website also records his death, confirms he died on MV *Neptunian* and that he was 'Son of William Hills Cuthbert and Elizabeth Henrietta Cuthbert, of North Shields, Northumberland'. He was only 16 and was serving as a Cabin Boy at the time of his death. The website at: http://www.uboat.net/index.html says that *Neptunian* was sailing with convoy SC-2 from North America to Liverpool, carrying 8,500 tons of sugar and that: 'At 04.04 hours on 7 Sep, 1940, the *Neptunian* (Master Alexander Thomas Campbell) in convoy SC-2 was hit by one torpedo from *U-47* north-west of Rockall and sank capsizing after seven minutes. The ship had been missed by one torpedo at 03.36 and 03.45 hours. The master and 35 crew members were lost.'

In looking at the medal record for Frank Tomaselli Cuthbert I noted, on the same page, reference to a Philip T Cuthbert, also born in North Shields. It seemed at least possible that this was another cousin, and so it proved to be. Born on 13 July 1920, his full name was Philip Tomaselli Cuthbert, which was a pleasant surprise. His record, in BT 382/2251, comprises several cards covering his service between 1941 and 1972, the cut-off date for the series. As he was only 52 it seems likely that he continued in the Merchant Marine after this date.

His BT 382 record commences with his being discharged from SS *Thistleford* on 24 August 1941; he joined *Rajahstan* on 3 September 1941 and served on her until May 1942; between July 1942 and May 1943 he was on *Empire Hazlitt*; between June 1943 and February 1944 he was on *Ocean Traveller*. For six weeks he was part of the Merchant Navy Reserve Pool (MNRP) and actually paid for waiting at home for a fresh ship (something that would not have occurred before the introduction of the Reserve Pool). In April 1944 he signed on to *Merton* and was on her until December. From January 1945 until June 1945 he was aboard *Fort Orleans*.

There are ships cards for these vessels in BT 389 series giving the name of a ship and details of its movements, i.e. the ports at which it docked, and passage between ports. They also record the location (latitude and longitude) and date on which a ship was sunk. The cards don't always reflect changes in the ship's name so you may find it necessary to search for a ship under its various names.

*Rajahstan* has a total of a dozen cards confirming she was owned by the Hindustan Steamship Company with a gross tonnage of 6,391 tons and details numerous sailings to West Africa and North America.

Merchant ships generally travelled in convoy under escort from the Royal Navy. A huge complex of convoy organisation ran around the globe. Surviving convoy records are in ADM 237 series but they are indexed by convoy number so are difficult to study with this. There is a card index at TNA which may provide the necessary details, though it's clear from looking for cards for some of the ships Philip Tomaselli Cuthbert sailed on, that not all ships are indexed. Some convoy records are indexed in the ADM 199 series so a search on this series using the ship's name might produce something. One or two of the ships that Philip Tomaselli Cuthbert served on appear using this search method, notably *Rajahstan* which made several trips across the North Atlantic in 1941/42, the height of the Battle of the Atlantic, when shipping casualties were at their highest. If you can't find a ship mentioned using this method then a search of the ADM 12 indexes (see Chapter 3 on the

Royal Navy) might produce references to mentions in ADM series files.

BT 347 series cards record the daily ship casualties mainly due to enemy action but also routine causes of losses at sea which affected allied merchant fleets during the Second World War. Each incident is recorded naming the class of vessel, the ship's name, nationality of the ship, date and time, cause and approximate position, voyage details and cargo and latest information available.

Due to the nature of the work the bodies of the vast majority of Merchant Navy casualties were never recovered. They are commemorated in the Second World War extension to the Tower Hill Memorial on the south side of the garden of Trinity Square, London, close to the Tower of London. The Memorial Register may be consulted at Trinity House Corporation, Trinity Square (Cooper's Row entrance), Tower Hill,

*Part of the Merchant Navy Memorial at Tower Hill.*

London, EC3N 4DH, which will be found behind the Memorial; tel: 02074 816900. It commemorates almost 24,000 men and women of the Merchant Marine.

As Winchester Diocese includes the major port of Southampton, Winchester Cathedral holds the Second World War Merchant Navy Book of Remembrance which may be examined on request.

A great deal of information on how to research individual ships and Merchant Marine sailors can be found at: http://www.mariners-l.co.uk.

There is a fascinating website containing images of many British merchant vessels from the Second World War at: http://www.photoship.co.uk.

A website devoted to the Merchant Navy in the Second World War with photographs and much information can be found at: http://www.second-worldwar.org.uk/merchantnavy.html.

*Chapter 7*

# THE HOME GUARD

Just after the early evening BBC news of 14 May 1940 the Secretary of State for War, Anthony Eden, made a speech to the nation. The war was not going well and the British Expeditionary Force was in full retreat towards Dunkirk.

> We want large numbers of . . . British subjects between the ages of seventeen and sixty-five to come forward and offer their services . . . You will not be paid but will receive uniforms and will be armed. In order to volunteer, what you have to do is give your name at your local police station, and then, when we want you, we will let you know.

Even before the broadcast was at an end, police stations were being besieged by volunteers. It was the beginning of the Local Defence Volunteers (LDV) soon to be renamed the Home Guard by Winston Churchill.

All across the country groups of men began to form up into units. Units were established on an ad hoc basis. Many factories established their own units. In 2nd Battalion, Dunbarton Home Guard, 'B' Company was drawn wholly from men employed at John Brown & Co. and 'C' Company from Works Units at the Ministry of Supply, Turners Asbestos Co. Ltd, Beardmore Diesels Ltd and other local companies. At Wilmington in Sussex the local men met in a farmyard after work. There were shepherds, shopkeepers, farmhands, a retired civil servant, a retired schoolteacher and one or two commuters who worked in London. The local publican was elected section leader because he was a good shot and always in the village. It also helped that his wife had access to a telephone because she worked at the local 'big house'.

Only 40 per cent of men had served previously, mostly during the First World War. Naturally these men tended to take up positions of responsibility. Because of the rapid creation of their units the volunteers generally took it upon themselves to appoint their own officers and NCOs. Some units held elections; in most, especially in rural areas, local landowners and officials took over. In many factory units the foremen and managers assumed the roles. A few units petitioned the military authorities to appoint officers.

The duties of the local units initially comprised the manning of fixed defences around vital positions such as bridges and viaducts, patrolling against German paratroop or seaborne landings and the manning of road blocks. Quite naturally, they also helped out the Civil Defence teams in the event of air raids.

In late 1941 some Home Guard units were given an anti-aircraft role because the troops of Anti-Aircraft Command were being transferred to regular units for service overseas. By March 1942 over 11,000 Home Guard were being trained to man guns and searchlights and the numbers grew as the war progressed.

Though the Home Guard is thought of as an all-male preserve there were always women associated with the units, performing the vital tasks of providing refreshments and administration. In 1943 a Women's Auxiliary was formed to recognise these invaluable women. Though not permitted a uniform, they were allowed a badge and many enlisted, though just as many preferred to just get on with doing what they had been without all the fuss.

Following a parade in London the Home Guard were stood down on 3 December 1944, and the whole Home Guard was officially disbanded on 31 December 1945. Shortly after their creation their numbers had reached 1.5 million and their numbers never fell below 1 million throughout the war. As the minimum age for the Home Guard was 17 and the Army 18, many young men spent a formative part of their military service in the Home Guard having been conscripted in as a way of introducing them to military life.

## Home Guard Medals

Men who had served in the Home Guard for three years or more were entitled to the Defence Medal, but had to apply for it.

Because they didn't come face to face with the enemy the Home Guard were not entitled to the Victoria Cross, but two members were posthumously awarded the George Cross. One was Section Commander G W Inwood who, on the night of 15/16 October 1940, with a party of volunteers helped police dig out survivors from a gas-filled cellar after an air raid. Inwood volunteered to enter the cellar through a small hole and rescued two men. On his third attempt he was dragged out exhausted and collapsed. In spite of the best efforts of medical staff he died shortly afterwards. His widow was presented with his George Cross in 1941. The other recipient was 61-year-old Lieutenant W Foster of the Wiltshire Home Guard who threw himself on a hand grenade during practice, when it fell into a trench full of men.

In total, 137 medals for bravery were awarded to Home Guard personnel. If you think a relative may have received such an award then a search of the *London Gazette* may give you a date and the local paper will almost certainly cover the story. Some recommendations may appear in the AIR 2 series of records of the Civilian Gallantry Awards Committee. Many officers and men received awards for good service, most of which will appear in the New Year's Honours List or King's Birthday Honours List and which appear in the *London Gazette*.

## Home Guard Personal Records

Individual records for Home Guard members are still retained by the Ministry of Defence but they can be released to the member himself, or to next of kin, on application to the Army Personnel Centre, Historic Disclosures, Mailpoint 400, Kentigern House, 65 Brown Street, Glasgow, G2 8EX; tel: 08456 009663. Details on how to do this can be found online at: http://www.army .mod.uk/documents/general/hg_info.pdf, which also explains about data protection and charges made for searching for records.

The information held on individual Home Guards is very limited, normally consisting of one double-sided A4 sheet of paper (Army Form W3066) containing personal details on enlistment and very little else. No details are held of the duties performed by an individual during his service.

There have been apparently well-informed rumours for several years that Home Guard records are going to be released to TNA and opened without restriction. This release is still under negotiation so you should contact Glasgow for the time being.

TNA holds copies of the *Home Guard List* on its open shelves in their Microfilm Reading Room. As with the *Army List*, this deals exclusively with officers, but the *Home Guard List* does, at least, tell you which unit the officer served with.

## Home Guard Unit Records

Home Guard units weren't required to keep war diaries but many did so anyway, particularly when their officers had served in the First World War and were used to doing so. TNA holds a lot of unit histories and unofficial war diaries in its WO 199 (Home Defence) records. Some of the unit histories contain interesting and amusing anecdotes about the life and role of the average Home Guard member. You can search for material relating to units in the area in which your relative served using TNA's general search engine. The record for the Anglesey Home Guard is, for example, in WO 199/3311 recording significant events such as their officers' dinner, held on the night of 2 December 1944, at the Masonic Hall, Beaumaris at which thirty battalion officers attended and sent a telegram of loyalty and affection to the King. The next day a 'Stand Down' parade was held in the town hall at which speeches of thanks were made and the lady auxiliaries provided tea.

WO 199 also includes many policy files relating to relations between the Home Guard and the Regular Army and government. If you can't find records at TNA then try the museum of the local regiment as many Home Guard units came under the territorial organisation and counted as regi-mental battalions. The local record office or library is likely to hold at least some material (Swindon Library holds an excellent GWR Home Guard album containing many photographs) and the local press will usually be a good source. Because many of the volunteers were very young it is possible that some members of local units are still alive and can be traced.

There's an excellent website dealing with the general history of the Home Guard at: http://www.home-guard.org.uk and there are an increasing number of sites that deal specifically with local units.

Large amounts of information on local Home Guard units may be traced using Access to Archives (see p. 8) which links to local archives nationwide. Using this it's possible to find, for example, that Bolton Archive and Local Studies Service hold a series of pamphlets, forms, orders and expense sheets, as well as some lists of individuals, relating to the Lancashire Home Guard; likewise, Somerset Archive and Record Service hold two group photographs of Taunton Home Guard and other material relating to Somerset in general.

## The Home Guard Auxiliary Units

The probability of German invasion in 1940 prompted the creation of a highly secret organisation, nominally linked to the Home Guard, to act clandestinely in support of the Regular Army by conducting sabotage behind enemy lines. Secret Service officers went quickly to work recruiting 'clergymen, game-keepers, poachers, dentists and road-menders in defence of their country'. They began their recruitment drive in early June 1940 and by late July had appointed nearly 200 key men and established over 1,000 dumps of explosives and incendiary materials.

By the third week of July the invasion still looked likely, but plans for defence were well in hand. The Army had begun to establish its own stay-behind units, on a rather more formal military basis, designed to fight in close cooperation with the Army and newly formed Home Guard. The two sets of units were merged under the command of Colonel Colin Gubbins and more men were recruited, usually from the Home Guard, and were named GHQ Auxiliary Units.

The Headquarters of the Auxiliary Units was at Coleshill House near Swindon. Here they were trained in unarmed combat, handling explosives and night scouting. Mail for HQ was addressed via the post office at nearby Highworth and visitors would call there first to be picked up by car. The local postmistress, Mabel Stranks, would call through to Coleshill to let them know that they had visitors and an unmarked vehicle would arrive to carry them up to the house. It was a vital 'cut-out' between the organisation and the outside world.

Patrols were recruited locally and operated under conditions of great secrecy, usually from carefully concealed underground bunkers. They weren't supposed to fight the Germans but to carry out sabotage against communications and supply dumps in support of Regular Army units. Their life expectancy was not reckoned to be high in the event the Germans managed to get established.

To explain why the Auxiliaries could wear Home Guard uniforms but not be part of their local units, three nominal battalions were created to which the men were attached. GHQ Special Reserve Battalion 201 covered Scotland and the North of England; 202 Battalion covered the Midlands and 203 the southern counties.

The Auxiliary Units were stood down in April 1945 and formally disbanded in July 1945; some of their younger members had already transferred to the Regular Army, including the Special Air Service.

## Special Duties Section

Not all the Auxiliaries transferred to Gubbins' command. A secret report says: 'it is still considered necessary that the intelligence side of its activities should be maintained and developed'. These men and women continued to work clandestinely as Auxiliary Units (Special Duties) section, never wearing a uniform and staying in contact with HQ by secret means. It appears that these people were considered as part of the Secret Intelligence Service (what we now call MI6) so it's highly unlikely that records of their activities will ever be released.

## Auxiliary Unit Records

The few surviving files relating specifically to the Auxiliary Units can generally be found under the WO 199 (Home Forces) reference (try searching in WO 199 using the keyword 'Auxiliary'). Most of the organisation's files are said to have been lost in a fire that destroyed Coleshill House in the late 1940s. Some files on the early days of the organisation went to SOE with Gubbins and can be found in the HS series at TNA.

For those seeking a relative who may have served with the Auxiliary Units there are three lists of men in WO 199/3388, WO 199/3389 and WO 199/3390 dating from about the end of 1943. WO 199/3391 is a handwritten register of men who served in the southern counties. These lists don't seem to include members of the Special Duties Section.

A museum dedicated to the Auxiliaries was established at Parham in Suffolk in 1997 alongside the museum to the 390th Bomb Group Memorial Air Museum. It has an extensive collection of artefacts donated by members and their relatives including various original and copy weapons (some of the coshes, knives and garrottes have been recreated by veteran patrol members based on their original designs from 1940). The museum has over 200 photographs of original patrols, which might aid relatives trying to find out if an ancestor served, as well as over 40 tape recordings of veterans reminiscing. Their extensive network of contacts, throughout the country, is made up of experts on patrols in their own local area. The Museum is always keen to hear from former patrol members and their relatives.

There's been an increased interest in the work of the Auxiliary Units over the last twenty years and there are some fascinating websites relating to the whole organisation or to individual units. http://bsswebsite.me.uk/Local-history/HomeGuardAU/HomeGuardAU.html has a brief history of the patrols in the Ledbury area of Herefordshire. http://www.brandonatwar .co.uk/aux_unit.htm details the patrol at Brandon, Suffolk (with a list of patrol members). The Coleshill Auxilliary Research Team have a very useful website featuring histories, illustrations and a user forum at: http://www.coleshillhouse.com. The website of the British Resistance Museum at Parham is at: http://www.parhamairfieldmuseum.co.uk/ brohome.html.

# Chapter 8

# SECRET ORGANISATIONS

The Second World War was a war won as much by intelligence as by brute force and overwhelming strength. The intelligence and sabotage organisations that were so incredibly secret during the war and during the cold war have, gradually, shed some of their secrecy and, with the deliberate exception of MI6 (the overseas secret service), have released at least some of their files.

## MI5

Responsible for security in Britain and the Empire, MI5 was a top-secret organisation under the authority of the Home Secretary, though with extensive military connections (hence the Military Intelligence nomenclature). Having been a very small organisation before the war (only 26 officers in January 1938), it grew rapidly to employ 332 officers by January 1943.

Tracing MI5 ancestors before the Second World War is relatively easy. KV 1/59 is a chronological staff list up to December 1919 (several staff are known to have served in both world wars). It's not alphabetic, so it may take time to trace an individual. Other lists in KV 1 show the MI5 sections individuals worked in. KV 4/127 contains surviving staff lists up until the end of 1939. No complete staff list from the Second World War period has yet been released.

There are occasional part lists of officers and staff scattered through the released papers (KV 4/19 has one) and it is to be hoped that further lists will be released in the future.

Postings to MI5 should appear as such on an officers' service record, usually to MI5, possibly to Room 055 War Office (an MI5 cover), though you may find some noted as Port Control Officers (who ran security at the ports for MI5). A good many Intelligence Corps men were seconded to MI5 for a variety of duties.

MI5 employed a large number of secret agents for keeping an eye on suspect organisations such as the Communist Party and Fascist organisations, as well as reporting on individuals. It's very rare to find them mentioned, especially under their real names. There's an interesting list of MI5 agents working against German and Japanese organisations abroad in KV 4/163 which only gives their cover names but drops enough hints that might allow you to identify some of them. MI5 ran agents on British-based merchant ships calling at foreign ports to keep an eye on Merchant Seamen abroad and to watch for German attempts to recruit them as agents. Several of these agents are actually named under their real names.

## The Government Code & Cypher School (Bletchley Park)

GC&CS was the top-secret organisation that monitored and deciphered foreign communications and was a vital part of Britain's intelligence organisation, deciphering German codes. During the Second World War it was officially part of the Secret Intelligence Service but became a separate organisation, Government Communications Headquarters (GCHQ) after the war. Records from Bletchley Park are released to TNA under their HW series. Some 10,000 men and women served at Bletchley during the course of the war, some working on radio interception, some on deciphering (using an increasingly complex range of machines, including the first ever computer), translation and analysis. Staff were explicitly forbidden to discuss their work with the public at the time, and after they left – and this code of silence was maintained until the early 1970s when a former officer published a book that set out some of Bletchley's successes. This gradually meant that other people felt able to come forward, particularly after the government admitted to Bletchley's role, though many continued to hold to their silence.

### Tracing Bletchley Park Staff

No complete contemporary list of Bletchley Park staff is known to have survived. There are some surviving section staff lists in TNA's HW series. HW 14/9 contains a December 1940 list of all GC&CS personnel, excluding those engaged in British cipher production at Mansfield College, Oxford. It's in alphabetical order and lists the huts staff served in, staff serving in radio interception stations and out-stations such as Wavendon, Denmark Hill and Sandridge. Sometimes, where their duties were not immediately related to code breaking, there's a detail of their work – Mrs D I Arthur is a typist at Wavendon, Mr F W Buckingham an office keeper at the school and Private D Phillips is a motor driver attached to Hut 5.

HW 14/16 covers the organisation of Hut 3, which housed the analysts who interpreted the material deciphered in Hut 6 in June 1941. Numerous members of the naval, military and civilian staff are named and their specialisms noted. A final list gives details of the personnel of Hut 3, which was closely linked to Hut 6, including the Army other ranks and the female ATS and civilian staff.

Searches on TNA's website for HW files with the words staff or personnel in their descriptions can be productive. HW 14/36 contains the description 'GCCS partial staff listing; staffing of AS' and it contains two short lists from

1942, one of ten WRNS who had been posted away and a list of some sixty-three technical officers and their assistants, complete with dates of birth.

HW 41/219 contains comprehensive nominal rolls and staff postings of various field signals intelligence units from 1945, listing many hundreds of soldiers who worked either on field interception duties or in the units that transmitted and received the Ultra decrypts.

By September 1942 there were over 2,000 staff at Bletchley and papers relating to them concentrate increasingly on shortages and ways of dealing with them. More military personnel came in, particularly WRNS, WAAF and ATS women, whose service has not been recorded. If you can obtain their service record then there's no reason why service at GC&CS should not be released by the relevant service records office. Postings might be shown as to SLU (Special Liaison Units), FSIU (Field Signals Intelligence Units) or GCHQ (Government Communications Headquarters).

### The Bletchley Park Personnel Master List

A volunteer at Bletchley has compiled a two-part list of staff. Part I, drawn from contemporary wartime documents, contains some 3,800 names, along with details of the document that named them. Part II is derived from non-official sources, in particular the Heritage Service Forms that veteran visitors are requested to complete when they visit Bletchley. There's some duplication in the lists and the possibility of error, but this list remains the most comprehensive roll of Bletchley Park staff.

Bletchley Park is now open to the public, with a fascinating museum and tours given by dedicated volunteers. Their archive contains much original material though little on individuals apart from their excellent Personnel Master List. They are always keen to hear from former staff and their relatives and to obtain details of their service. Their website is at: http://www
.bletchleypark.org.uk.

## Special Operations Executive (SOE)

Special Operations Executive (SOE) was the secret organisation responsible for 'setting Europe ablaze', in Churchill's words. With Nazi occupation of most of Europe SOE was formed by amalgamating the Army's MIR section (which looked at irregular warfare generally) and the Secret Service's (MI6) Section D, which was looking after sabotage and black propaganda.

Though mainly known for their operations dropping agents into occupied Europe to help the resistance organisations, SOE was actually a worldwide network with men and women working to counter Axis operations in many neutral countries.

No comprehensive list of SOE agents and staff appears to exist, though the surviving personnel files on many of them (probably by far the majority) have been released to TNA in their HS 9 series.

## The (Non) Missing Personnel Files

HS 9 series contains some 1,654 files, many of which contain details of more than 1 agent (HS 9/3 contains 11 agents). There are over 13,000 individual records in the series. Legend says that only 13 per cent of SOE's personnel files survive, many having been destroyed in a fire after the war. If this is the case then SOE must have had over 100,000 staff and agents, but this is patent nonsense – no organisation that large could function as a secret one for very long. M R D Foot's book *SOE – The Special Operations Executive 1940–46* states that 'SOE's total strength was never more than 10,000 men and 3,200 women', in which case almost all their files should survive. Yet there are certainly cases I've looked into that with further investigation show absolutely that the person was with SOE, but there is no HS 9 file.

Having run a random selection of names culled from the Imperial War Museum's extensive SOE collection against the HS 9 files I think that there is a greater than 75 per cent chance that the record of any given individual is likely to be findable, provided that they served with SOE within Britain at some point. Analysis of the SOE Index of Honours and Awards suggests that men and women recruited locally by SOE stations abroad are less likely to be in the HS 9 files (but it is always worth a check). The higher ranked the individual the less likely it is there will be a file and I suspect that records of many of the junior servicemen who were attached to SOE briefly for work in the field may not survive either. It is harder to trace women, partly because the fire does seem to have destroyed a section of the SOE archive housing their records, also because many will subsequently have married and their record will be in their maiden name. The files cover operational agents (men and women who dropped into Europe) as well as training and administrative staff, including senior officers such as Maurice Buckmaster who controlled the French Section and general dutymen at the various training schools.

Some of the personnel files have not been released because, as TNA's website rather coyly says, 'many PFs were transferred to the personal files maintained of other government agencies for which an individual agent subsequently worked'. It would be nice to think that, if you can't find a personnel file for someone you know was with SOE, they went on to work for MI6. Unfortunately, without other evidence you can't really take this as proof just, possibly, as indicative.

HS 9 records are fully searchable online using TNA's search engine and the indexing seems to be particularly thorough, including codenames of agents where known. Unless a staff member is known to be dead the file will be closed until 100 years have passed since their birth, though if you can prove they have died the file will be opened for you by applying online to TNA.

In addition to the HS 9 files there's a partial list of SOE employees, possibly compiled by George Courtauld, a director of the giant textile concern and a shipping magnate in his spare time. The list is in the form of a ledger, alphabetically organised, but chronologically within each letter, in HS 8/1013. Courtauld was one of SOE's senior headhunters who apparently got anything, or anyone, that Baker Street needed, any way that was required to get it. The list may well have started life as a list of MI6 Section D people as it certainly lists at least one MI6 officer (Claude Dansey) who isn't known to have had any SOE connections. The list contains about 6,000 names, many of them listed as domestic staff at SOE's many secret training schools, and at some point someone has carefully gone through the list noting how many of those named have surviving personnel files. At a rough estimate something between a third and one-half of those named don't have personnel files, the earlier they joined the less chance there is that they don't. If you believe that an ancestor served with SOE and there's no file in HS 9 then HS 8/1013 is certainly worth checking.

You may also wish to check the various SOE Section Record Cards (HS 12–HS 20), though it will greatly assist you if you have some idea of the part of the world they served in. Some Army (and presumably Navy and RAF personnel) who were attached to SOE may not be listed in SOE's records. If you can obtain their service records look out for references to SOE cover names such as SO2, Force 133, Force 136, Force 139 or the Inter Services Research Board (ISRB).

## The Secret Intelligence Service (SIS or MI6)

The Secret Intelligence Service (which used a cover name of MI6 during the Second World War, and this has stuck in the public imagination) was the foreign-intelligence arm of the secret service, running secret agents abroad and gathering military, political and economic intelligence that couldn't be acquired by normal means. Though throughout the 1920s and early 1930s its main target had been the Soviet Union, it always maintained an interest in Germany and ran agents there from bases in Holland, Switzerland and other adjoining countries.

Unlike MI5 and SOE the Secret Intelligence Service does not release information on its officers, staff or agents. Enquiries to the agency about people who might have worked for it are met with a polite refusal. When a former member of staff dies (I have this from the son of one of their former clerical staff) their estate receives a letter from the 'Foreign Office' (who pay for SIS) reminding them that any official papers they may have retained are government property which should be returned at once.

For SIS officers and staff working abroad during the Second World War, Passport Control, the Foreign Office visa system which operated offices in foreign countries, was frequently a 'cover'. When civilian staff went abroad they were provided with passports gratis by Passport Control and this appears alongside their entry in FO 610 (Passport Registers) series. Records are strictly chronological so you'll need to know roughly when they went abroad and then search carefully through the entries until you find theirs. This can take some time.

Other cover names used during the Second World War were MI6, ISLD (Inter Services Liaison Department) and GCB (Government Communications Bureau) which might appear on records. MI6 and ISLD are more likely to appear on an officer's service record, or possibly on an ordinary soldier seconded to SIS for, for example, working radio communications. GCB is more likely to appear on documents of civilian employees. There was a considerable interchange of staff between SIS and SOE, and a certain degree of interchange with MI5 so a check of their records might prove useful.

*Chapter 9*

# PRISONERS OF WAR

etween them Germany and Italy took a total of 142,319 British prisoners. Japan captured 50,016. There were, of course, many thousands of Commonwealth prisoners as well as American, Russian and other allies. The good news about having a prisoner of war (POW) relative is that there is probably more information openly available about prisoners of war than about any other category of serviceman in the Second World War.

If you weren't already aware that a relative had been a POW from either themselves or other relatives, don't necessarily expect to find much on any service record you receive from the MOD. Frequently all it will say is 'Missing' with a date, followed by 'Reported as POW by Red Cross' at a later date. At least you'll know that they spent some time as a POW and can begin searching for additional information.

## Basic Information

There are lists of POWs in TNA's WO 392 series between WO 392/1 and WO 392/26 and they're broken down by service, which makes searching a little easier; WO 392/1, for example, lists all known British Army POWs in the hands of the Germans in September 1944; WO 392/2 lists Australian soldiers in German hands at the same date; WO 392/7 lists naval personnel and WO 392/9 Merchant Navy. Others list New Zealanders, South Africans, Air Force personnel, Canadians and Indian Army prisoners. WO 392/11–WO 392/20 cover the same categories in April 1945. WO 392/21–WO 392/22 list the same categories of prisoner held by the Italians. WO 392/23–WO 392/26 are alphabetical lists of POWs held by the Japanese. These records are available through the DocumentsOnline section of TNA's website.

POW record cards for men captured by the Germans and Italians are still held by the MOD but a copy of an individual's card (subject to the standard release only to next of kin or the individual themselves) can be obtained from the Veterans Agency in Blackpool. The card is similar in design to the Japanese cards in TNA (see below), giving very much the same kind of information, including date and place of capture, camps held in and name and address of next of kin. Information is, unfortunately, often sparse.

## Life in POW Camps

Each camp had a Senior British Officer (SBO), or Vertrauensmann ('man of confidence')who was responsible for the internal administration of the prisoners themselves and for maintaining morale. He also acted as the main contact point with the enemy commander and his administration. In well-organised camps the SBO had a team of assistants.

The Geneva Convention did allow for prisoners to be made to work for their captors, though officers could not be forced to work at all, NCOs should only be given supervisory work and no one was allowed to be made to do work they were physically unfit for. There was to be regular time off, hours should be equivalent to similar civilian workers and there should be compensation for industrial accidents. Prisoners were not allowed to work on anything connected with the war. Of course, given the circumstances, this didn't always happen. Germany was particularly short of labour and local employers were allowed to approach POW camps to obtain working parties. The men were paid, but only in a special currency that could be spent in the camp.

For many prisoners the main problem was boredom. The routines of the camp provided some relief, with regular roll calls, sick parades, meal times and arrival of mail. The Red Cross managed to provide some books for camp libraries and parcels from home.

## Prisoner of War Interrogation Questionnaires

A key source of information on individual POWs from all the services consists of the Interrogation Questionnaires that the majority of them completed in 1945. A top-secret organisation called MI9 (part of the Secret Service) was set up to help them escape and to train them in avoiding capture. Towards the end of the war MI9 set about a mass interrogation of prisoners as they were released and compiled a general questionnaire that each man was required to complete. The reports are held alphabetically in WO 344 series.

This series consists of approximately 140,000 Liberation Questionnaires completed by mainly British and Commonwealth POWs of all ranks and services, plus a few other Allied nationals and Merchant Seamen. While the plans to question all liberated POWs never materialised, these records nevertheless represent a large percentage of those still in captivity in 1945.

As well as giving personal details, name, rank, number, unit and home address, these records can include: date and place of capture; main camps and hospitals in which imprisoned and work camps; serious illnesses suffered while a prisoner and any medical treatment received; interrogation after capture; escape attempts; sabotage; suspicion of collaboration by other Allied prisoners; details of bad treatment by the enemy to themselves or others.

Individuals were also given the opportunity to bring to official notice courageous acts by fellow prisoners or details of civilians who assisted them during escape and evasion activities.

Questionnaires also enquire if the prisoner had witnessed or had any information about war crimes. If so, they were required to complete a form 'Q'. These forms contained information about behaviour of enemy captors that could constitute illegal acts.

WO 344/1 to WO 344/359 contain reports on POWs of the Germans; WO 344/360 contains miscellaneous reports A to W including Army, Navy, RAF, air personnel other than RAF, Marines, Merchant Navy and civilians; WO 344/361–WO 344/410 contain questionnaires for POWs of the Japanese, again held alphabetically.

Most reports just list the camps the particular individual was held in, perhaps a little on the kind of work they were obliged to do, though in a reasonable proportion there's more detailed material. The questionnaire of Warrant Officer Ronald Mead RAF, captured when shot down over Italy in 1941, contains details of two escape attempts (one successful) and of a possible British collaborator with the Germans. It also contains reports on the shooting of Sergeant L H Stevenson RCAF by the Germans and details of how Jewish prisoners were segregated in one of the camps. The report of Sergeant Leonard Robson, captured with his Coastal Artillery Battery at Tobruk in 1942, contains a description of an escape attempt from the station at Graz. He managed to make his way into the hills but 'could only travel by night and the woods were full of German Home Guard, SS and German military, had very little food'. Hearing that the advancing Russians were getting close, he continued to lie up in the woods where he was met by a woman who brought him clothes and eventually hid him in the loft in her home. The SS commandeered rooms in her house, but she talked them out of searching the loft. After a period the SS left and a couple of days later the Russians arrived. Putting on his British uniform Sergeant Robson presented himself to a Russian officer, who accused him of having stolen the uniform and papers and threatened to have him shot. The woman then:

> offered herself to the officer to save me and he accepted, raping her. The next day we left the house and went next door with some old people and the woman had a heart attack and no doctor could come. As an Englishman I stayed and helped her get better till was picked up by the Russians, the day before I was going to the British lines.

## Camp Histories

At the end of the war a number of camp histories were compiled by all three services. For the Army these are in WO 208 series, for the RAF in AIR 40 and for the Royal Navy scattered through ADM 1 series. You can search for these reports using the camp name or number on TNA's website.

WO 208/3277 is the secret history of Stalag VIIIc at Kunau in Silesia. It describes how the first British prisoners were moved there from a camp in Italy in October 1943. By December 1944 the camp held 6,969 prisoners, mostly British but including Canadians, Australians, New Zealanders and over 1,000 South Africans and Indians. The camp had originally been used for Belgian, Russian and Serbian prisoners and it took a lot of disinfectant to rid it of lice and fleas. In January 1945 the camp was broken up because it was likely to be overrun by the advancing Russians and the prisoners sent to camps further west.

The history reports on living conditions in the camp, on mail received, leisure activities (football was allowed four times a week) and the work camps that came under Stalag VIIIc's control. The men worked in concrete factories, railway works, gasworks, in the Post Office, on tramways and on aerodromes. The history notes that 'Stalag VIIIc compared very favourably with other Stalags and the morale of P/W's was high throughout'.

Though there was no British escape committee some kind of organisation existed among French prisoners who provided French uniforms to men who wanted to get out of the British camp. Though some men may have got out in this way, no one managed to escape successfully.

The men did manage to build a radio receiver from parts brought in from Italy and from other parts 'acquired' by working parties and smuggled into the camp. The first BBC news was heard on 1 June 1944 and a regular newsletter was circulated among the men to counter German propaganda. The history says:

> The Germans suspected the presence of the wireless set and carried out weekly searches but never succeeded in finding it, as it was cleverly concealed in a biscuit tin which measured ten inches in height by three inches in width by 2 inches in depth. The tin was left lying on top of a pile of junk made up of other tins etc, and on one occasion while a search was being carried out, the tin containing the set was given to a German sentry to hold while the pile of rubbish was investigated.

## Escape Reports

It was a POW's duty to attempt to escape, though with the Channel between them and Britain and Sweden, Spain and Switzerland the only neutral countries they could get to for much of the war, it wasn't easy. When Italy switched sides in 1943 many POWs were able to escape (in fact many Italian guards just opened the gates and let them out). Escape reports, compiled by MI19, are in WO 208 series – WO 208/3298–3327 are reports 1940–5; WO 208/4238–WO 208/4276 cover escapes to Switzerland (organised alphabetically which makes searching easier); WO 208/4368–WO 208/4371 also cover escapes to Switzerland. A few of these have been digitised and are available online at TNA's DocumentsOnline.

# The Red Cross

The responsibility for recording and advising on prisoners came under the International Red Cross and all of their records are now centralised in Switzerland. The address for contact is: Archives Division & Research Service, International Committee of the Red Cross, 19 Avenue de la Paix, Geneva, CH-1202, Switzerland. Please be aware that records are only available to next of kin and that a research fee is chargeable. You will also need to provide as much information as you can on the prisoner – nationality, name, rank, regiment, date of birth are all useful aids.

The Red Cross carried out regular visits to camps to ensure that the terms of the Geneva Convention were being kept. Copies of these reports were sent to the British government and there are copies at TNA. Early reports (1939–41) are in FO 961 series, which also includes extensive papers and reports on civilian internees and British subjects living in occupied territory or interned in neutral countries, as well as enemy internees in Britain. Later reports (1941 onwards) are in WO 224 series 'War Office: International Red Cross and Protecting Powers (Geneva): Reports concerning Prisoner of War Camps in Europe and the Far East'. Reports include details of the German officials in each camp, the name of the 'man of confidence' and medical staff. There are usually also descriptions of living accommodation, health and medical conditions, hygiene, laundry, food and discipline. As well as the main camps there are reports on conditions in the many work detachments submitted in private by their men of confidence. A report dated 16/17 December 1944 on Stalag XVIIa includes complaints from the men of confidence of six work detachments, including failure to provide overalls, lack of recreational space, bullying by a German guard, short bread rations, lack of showers and disinfectant and a long waiting list of prisoners requiring dentures. Reports on Japanese camps tend to contain far less detail.

# Prisoners of the Japanese

Though British POWs had a tough time of it in Germany, particularly towards the end of the war, their comrades who fell into the hands of the Japanese suffered far more intensely. Beatings and physical punishments were part and parcel of the average Japanese soldier's life. An officer 'would personally beat the Sergeant Major, either with a blow from his hand or belt, or more likely with the flat of his sword. I have seen this on numerous occasions', wrote one prisoner. This culture of beating filtered down to the ordinary soldier who would not hesitate to take it out on the prisoners he controlled. 'Dependent on the mood of the guards, usually Koreans, decided whether you got away with a single blow from a bamboo cane or a wholesale beating up from a whole gang of them'. Japanese rations and medical provision for their own troops were also basic so that they usually took what they required themselves and left the rest for the prisoners. But, despite these reasons, their treatment of their prisoners was frequently inexcusably barbaric and contrary to the rules of war. If you discover that a relative was a prisoner of the Japanese expect to find some horrific accounts of suffering, illness, ill-treatment and death.

There are alphabetical lists of British POWs in Japanese hands in TNA's WO 392 series between WO 392/23 (A–D) and WO 392/26 (R–Z). Prisoner of War Questionnaires for prisoners of the Japanese are between WO 392/23 and WO 392/26.

Other nominal rolls are scattered about other series. There are a few nominal rolls of RAF prisoners held by the Germans in the AIR 40 series. AIR 40/263 and 264 are nominal rolls of prisoners held in Stalag Lufts I and IV. AIR 40/269 lists prisoners in Stalag Luft III; AIR 40/270 is from Stalag IIIA; AIR 40/272 is Stalag 17B; AIR 40/276 and 277 Stalag 357. AIR 40 1488–1491 cover Stalag Luft III and there is a roll of other ranks prisoners for repatriation. ADM 201/111 is a nominal roll of Royal Marine POWs held by the Germans.

WO 367 contains three registers recording the names of some 13,500 Allied POWs and civilian internees of British and other nationalities. These give minimal information about each prisoner and were apparently compiled for the Japanese camp administration, although the majority of the information is given in English.

The registers refer to camps numbered 1–4 which are believed to refer to:

No. 1 POW camp – Changi
No. 2 POW camp – Serangoon Road Camp
No. 3 POW camp – River Valley Road Camp
No. 4 POW camp – Adam Road Camp.

Across each two-page spread information in respect of each prisoner is given under the following headings: on the left-hand page: name; registration card no.; rank; unit; occupation (service or previous civilian). On the right-hand page: registration card no. (repeated); dispersal, i.e. where the prisoners were sent.

There is Nominal Roll of RAF prisoners held at the notorious Changi Camp in Singapore in AIR 40, between AIR 40/1899 and AIR 40/1906.

## Prisoner of War Record Cards

TNA holds record cards for British POWs in the Far East in their WO 345 series, consisting of some 56,000 pre-printed cards which were compiled by an unknown central Japanese authority with some degree of Allied assistance. The cards record the following details:

Camp (in Japanese)
Name

Nationality (in English, or English and Japanese)
Rank (in English, or English and Japanese)
Place of capture (in English, or English and Japanese)
Father's name
Place of origin
Destination of report (assumed to be report of capture, sent to next of kin at address given)
Prisoner's camp number (in Japanese)
Date of birth
Unit and service number
Date captured (in English, or English and Japanese)
Mother's name
Occupation (in English, or English and Japanese)
Remarks
Other information (on reverse) which may include medical details (in Japanese, possibly partly translated).

Diagonal red lines across a card indicate that the prisoner died in captivity. Though I've never tried to have a card translated I am advised that in the vast majority of cases the information is purely administrative.

## Japanese War Crimes Relating to Prisoners of War

After the war there were a series of investigations into Japanese war crimes, particularly relating to ill-treatment in POW camps. WO 356 series (on microfilm in TNA's Open Reading Room) contains a series of index cards relating to prisoners, the accused, victims and witnesses and the camps themselves. WO 357 series contains record cards covering war crimes in the Far East; the assessment of evidence; the dispersal and disposal of suspects; the progress and outcome of trials; details of sentences; and the prison records of convicted people.

The cards include the names of Japanese tried, executed and imprisoned as well as those who couldn't be interrogated or tried because they had died. Unfortunately, with few exceptions, these cards are not of any use as indexes to other records. If you know, however, the camps your ancestor was imprisoned in, you can at least reckon that there are records to be located. There are records of incidents and conditions in POW camps in WO 325, which you can search using TNA's website, though many files are merely indexed by general location, such as Java or Sumatra, Netherlands East Indies or Burma–Siam railway, so be prepared for some long searches, and to reading sometimes quite harrowing material.

## Other Sources for Prisoners of War

There is a basic guide to TNA's records of POWs available on line at: http://www.nationalarchives.gov.uk/catalogue/RdLeaflet.asp?sLeafletID =303.

The Imperial War Museum has extensive collections of personal accounts of prisoners, as well as drawings and other works of art they produced, printed books, photographs and film. The IWM website is at: http:// london.iwm.org.uk.

A smaller collection of prisoner recollections is held at Leeds University in the Liddle Collection (from which many of the accounts in this article are drawn). These can be searched at: http://www.leeds.ac.uk/library/ spcoll/liddle/index.htm.

Ancestry.com provides access to a database of British POWs held by the Germans during the Second World War including basic information about which camps they were sent to, the POW number and the types of camp they were in.

The website at: http://www.bbc.co.uk/ww2peopleswar features stories compiled by the BBC from POWs themselves.

The website at: http://home.clara.net/clinchy/neeball.htm is dedicated to POW escapees and the organisations in Belgium that assisted them.

### Case Study – Chief Petty Officer Charles Halme Rogers: Mentioned in Despatches and a Prisoner of the Japanese

Charles Halme Rogers was from Swindon and served in the Royal Navy for nearly twenty-five years. He wrote a short booklet 'Final Action of HMS *Li-Wo* near Banka Island' describing his participation in a Victoria Cross action off Singapore in early 1942 and his escape to Sumatra, where he was captured by the Japanese.

He describes how, with Singapore on the verge of falling to the Japanese, he was ordered to take a party of men to join the *Li-Wo*, a patrol vessel of 1,000 tons armed with a 4in gun (with only 13 practice shells) and 2 Lewis guns. He was ordered to: 'detail off gun crews, lookouts and men for the engine and boiler rooms'. Escaping with great difficulty from Singapore, *Li-Wo* sighted a Japanese convoy, escorted by a cruiser and a destroyer.

Despite being heavily outnumbered, the Captain attacked the largest merchant ship in the convoy:

> Battle ensigns were hoisted . . . we closed rapidly with the 4" gun ready to fire . . . the first salvo fell short, the second crossed the bow and the third scored a direct hit just under the bridge. She appeared to be on fire and turned to port. The other ships turned to starboard and commenced firing at us with small calibre guns . . . The damaged ship was now approaching *Li-Wo*, still firing, so the CO decided to ram her. We hit her

at top speed amidships and became interlocked, our bows bucked back – we were now really at close quarters. A machine gun duel took place which was fast and furious, with many men being killed or wounded. The *Li-Wo* gunners eventually wiped out two guns which caused the Japanese to abandon ship, which by this time was well on fire.

Disentangling *Li-Wo* they set course away from the cruiser, zig-zagging as her shells fell closer and closer. Shrapnel caused many casualties, including Charles, who suffered three minor wounds.

After about the ninth salvo we were told to abandon ship, so all who were able to jumped overboard . . . The last sight I had of the *Li-Wo* as she started on her last voyage to the bottom of the ocean was something I shall never forget – her ensigns were still flying and the Captain was standing on the bridge and, although she was listing to port she was still under way. Then, suddenly she disappeared, the *Li-Wo* was no more. For this action Lt Thomas Wilkinson was awarded the Victoria Cross posthumously.

Charles saw a Japanese ship ram a lifeboat, then attack survivors in the water. It: 'circled around and opened a murderous attack with machine guns, hand grenades, coal and wood . . . Amidst the hell, men could be heard crying out for mercy, but still the Japanese continued their 'sport'. I lay on my back with my arms outstretched and luckily no shot came in my direction.'

The ship eventually moved away and the remaining survivors struggled towards the damaged and half submerged lifeboat:

There were no oars, food or medical supplies, all we could do was let the boat drift . . . We spent a very cold night and as dawn broke one of the officers whom I'd been holding in my arms, died from his severe shrapnel wounds. I informed Lt Stanton who helped me take off his lifebelt and put him over the side where he slowly sank below the surface.

Some members of the boat crew died, others swam off to try for land or ships in the distance. The three remaining men boarded another damaged lifeboat and raised the sail. They took in tow two liferafts with men aboard and sailed for Sumatra. Eventually, having avoided a Japanese patrol boat, they landed on the island of Banka. Unfortunately, so did the Japanese and they were, eventually, captured.

## Life as a Japanese Prisoner of War

In common with most POWs Charles completed an MI9 questionnaire, in WO 344/399/2, saying he was captured on 16 February 1942 at Muntok Banka

Island. Between 17 February and 18 April 1942 he was held at Muntok Hospital and then transferred to Chung Wha School Camp. On 20 June 1942 he was transferred to Mulo School Camp, on 15 July to Chung Wha Camp and finally on 4 April 1944 to Sungron Camp.

It's clear, from a letter in Charles effects, that there had been a war crimes trial for many of the officers and camp guards. A friend wrote to him in 1991 giving the names of many guards (including their nicknames among the prisoners) and details of their sentences. Among these were Lieutenant Yamakawa, camp rations officer and a guard named Ohara (nicknamed 'Gladys'), both of whom were said to have been executed.

There are index cards relating to Japanese war trials in the files of the Judge Advocate General in WO 353–WO 357, which between them index the camps, witnesses, suspects, trials and sentences for a series of war crimes trials. Unfortunately, as TNA's website admits, 'With few exceptions, these cards are not of any use as indexes to other records.' They do at least confirm some points, including the existence of Charles' camps and of Yamakawa and Ohara.

Records relating to many Far East war crimes trials are in WO 325 series, including investigations into incidents, and conditions in POW camps. To some extent these are searchable if you have the names of camps or, at least, their location. Unfortunately, there are no immediate references to Charles' camps so I was obliged to search several files before locating a record. This is WO 325/95 'Charges and verdicts against Japanese war criminals'. As well

*Record card for Japanese war criminal Ohara, otherwise known as 'Gladys' or 'The Irish Nip'.*

as listing the accused it gives details of the charges and an abstract of the evidence against them which gives information supporting the charges: 'The ill treatment took the various forms of mass beatings up by the Korean guards, individual beatings up using fists, feet, sticks, rifle butt and any weapons at hand, exposure of Prisoners in mass parades held at night for long periods without adequate clothing'. Allegations were also made that the rice ration was reduced twice and:

> was considerably less than that received by Japanese garrison troops and clearly was insufficient to maintain health. A disturbing factor . . . is that for a sick prisoner already undernourished, to cease working and enter hospital meant he lost his heavy duty rations and received a daily maximum of 200 g. rice. This was tantamount to a death sentence and . . . many instances occurred of men working until the very day they died. Sometimes a man would be buried in the very grave he had dug the day before . . . Prisoners rations were sold, given away, stolen and fed to animals . . . Prisoners were forced to eat snakes, lizards and insects . . . on one occasion when some men were cooking a dog, a guard discovered them and they were beaten and tortured . . . Nearly three hundred Prisoners died between Jan 1 and Sept 20 1945. The evidence of the Prisoners of War Doctors will show that these deaths resulted from malnutrition and from disease with malnutrition as the basic cause.

The Commanding Officer was accused of stealing Red Cross parcels, forcing working parties to work an 18-hour day and forbidding prisoners from using air-raid shelters. Dr Nakai, 'a weak inefficient, vain little man', was accused of allowing the sick to be housed with no blankets, mattresses or mosquito nets. 'Sanitation was primitive and conditions particularly in the dysentery ward were so horrible that the witness Mr Robinson who worked in that ward had to leave after his first visit, to vomit'. On at least four occasions Korean guards beat up patients within the hospital. Despite the protests of British doctors, Dr Nakai insisted on bringing dysentery cases into the camp without isolating them, resulting in the disease becoming endemic. 'When a naval rating Usher broke his back while working, Surgeon Lt Read asked Nakai for plaster of paris. Nakai gave him a roll of elastoplast. Usher will never walk again.'

Of the 24 accused, 1 or 2 were acquitted but 9 were sentenced to death by hanging, including Lieutenant Yamakawa and the guard Ohara. A total of 3 were imprisoned for life, 3 to 20 years and the remainder to terms between 3 and 18 years.

In 1946 Charles, who'd shrunk from 13 to 8 stone during his captivity, returned to Swindon, where he remained an active member of the Royal Naval Association until his death.

*Chapter 10*

# THE HOME FRONT

Everyone, by necessity, played their part in the Second World War; this was total war and the British Isles were, effectively, under siege for much of it. National Service compelled men and women into the armed forces or into war work in the fields or factories. Children were evacuated from the major cities through fear of bombing. Many people held down full-time jobs and also served in the Home Guard or on Civil Defence duties. Everyone had a Ration Book entitling them to a prescribed amount of rationed food.

Britain was considerably less centrally organised during the Second World War than it is now, so that most detailed Civil Defence and other aspects of civilian life were coordinated from London but organised on a regional and local level. Even the Home Guard, which became a national force, was originally created by groups of volunteers responding locally to a national radio broadcast. There were many more police forces than there are now, not only county forces but borough forces for quite small towns, and there was, of course, no National Health Service and hospitals and medical services were either private, charitable or run by local authorities. This means that if you're seeking information on someone who wasn't in the armed forces or working directly for central government, or just information on what was happening locally, you'll have to cast your net wide. TNA catalogue is always a good place to start, but records there are almost all of central government, frequently just collating statistics or directing overall policy, so expect to have to look elsewhere. The local archives may well have much material and many have now got online catalogues; you can run a search through Access to Archives service which can be accessed through TNA's website.

## National Service, the 1939 'Census' and Reserved Occupations

The National Service Act of 1939 set up a national register of everyone in the country, including their age, sex, address, occupation, marital status and whether they had already volunteered for National Service. A census was taken in September 1939 and on the basis of the information people were provided with Identity Cards and Ration Books and could be instructed to

# MINISTRY OF LABOUR AND NATIONAL SERVICE

## EMERGENCY POWERS (DEFENCE) ACTS, 1939-1941.

### DIRECTION ISSUED ON BEHALF OF THE MINISTER OF LABOUR AND NATIONAL SERVICE UNDER REGULATION 58A OF THE DEFENCE (GENERAL) REGULATIONS, 1939.

Note.—Any person failing to comply with a direction under Regulation 58A of the Defence (General) Regulations, 1939, is liable on summary conviction to imprisonment for a term not exceeding three months, or to a fine not exceeding £100 or to both such imprisonment and such fine. Any person failing to comply after such a conviction is liable on a further conviction to a fine not exceeding five pounds for every day on which the failure continues.

To *Mr Albert Ernest Leevett. Employment Exchange.*
*1 School Road,*      CHELTENHAM
*Charlton Kings.*      Date   8 - JUL '42

In pursuance of Regulation 58A of the Defence (General) Regulations, 1939, I, the undersigned, a National Service Officer within the meaning of the said Regulations, do hereby direct you to perform the services specified by the schedule hereto, being services which, in my opinion, you are capable of performing.

If you become subject to the provisions of an Essential Work Order in the employment specified in the schedule, the direction will cease to have effect and your right to leave the employment will be determined under that Order. Otherwise, this direction continues in force until withdrawn by a National Service Officer or until the employer specified in the schedule dispenses with your services.

I hereby withdraw all directions previously issued to you under Regulation 58A of the said Regulations and still in force.

*Gordon Brown,*
National Service Officer.

## SCHEDULE.

Employment as a labourer with Messrs. Sir A.MacAlpine & Co. Ltd. at Corsham, Wilts., beginning on the 14th day of July, 1942, particulars of which are as follows:-
   The rate of remuneration and conditions of service will be one shilling and fivepence three-farthings per hour at commencement for a 47 hour week, plus a bonus of twopence per hour when working beneath the surface. Over time when worked to be paid for at standard overtime rates.
   To report to the Ministry of Labour and National Service Site Office, Corsham, at 4 p.m. on Monday, 13th July, 1942.

E.D. 383 (Revised).      Wt. 48376/527 50M 2/42 C.N.&Co.Ltd. 749 (7244)
                              Wt. 8765/1112 100M 4/42 C.N.&Co.Ltd. 749 (7849)

*A Ministry of Labour and National Service directive ordering the subject to report for work as a labourer.*

attend tribunals that could oblige them to enlist in the armed forces or undertake war work in specific industries, Civil Defence or the Home Guard. Information collected on each person was: name, sex, date of birth, marital status, occupation, whether they were a member of the armed forces or reserves. The number issued with each Ration Book later became the National Health Service identity number for the person so the original records of the census are now held by the NHS Information Centre. A Freedom of Information Act ruling in 2009 gives limited access to the records but only in respect of people who appear in it and are now dead. For addresses in England and Wales (the search is done by address) there is a charge of £42 (with no refund for an unsuccessful search); contact: NHS Information Centre, The 1939 Register Team, Smedley Hydro Rm B108, Trafalgar Road, Birkdale, Southport, PR8 2HH. You will need to be able to prove that the person you are searching for is already dead.

For Scotland the charge is considerably less, £13, but this is for a person search, not an address search. Evidence of the death of the person who is the subject of the enquiry is required if the death of the person was not registered in Scotland. Applications should be sent to: General Register Office for Scotland, New Register House, Edinburgh, EH1 3YT; you can pay by cheque or credit card.

The government listed some occupations as vital to the war effort and men and women who worked in them were exempt from conscription. These included dock workers, shipyard workers, miners, farmers (though not agricultural workers as such), scientists, Merchant Seamen, railwaymen, most policemen and workers in the public utilities (gas, electricity and water). Both of my grandfathers were in reserved occupations – Granda Armstrong was a coal miner (though he did serve as a Fire Watcher in Newcastle on a voluntary basis) and Granda Tomaselli worked in the Tyne shipyards (and went to sea on *HMS King George V* when she returned to Scapa Flow after a refit in the Tyne).

Pen & Sword publish generic books on researching both coal miners, railway workers, police officers and shipyard workers in their 'Tracing Your Ancestors' series, which may provide useful clues on finding information about family members.

## Conscientious Objectors

There was considerably more sympathy, at least in official circles, for Conscientious Objectors (COs) in the Second World War than in the First World War. Even before the outbreak of war men could register as COs through the Ministry of Labour and National Service, though they were obliged to appear before local tribunals to make their case. There were seventeen regional tribunals established across the country.

Some 59,000 people attempted to register but the tribunals had the authority to register them conditionally, i.e. to impose conditions on them that allowed the government to direct them into agricultural or Civil Defence work. Nearly half the people who applied (28,720) were granted a conditional exemption from military service; 14,700 were directed into the armed forces but allowed to serve in a non-combatant role (including the Non Combatant Corps). Some 3,577 were granted unconditional exemption – so that about 12,200 were rejected and could be conscripted into the armed forces or directed into war work.

Though the minutes and judgements of the tribunals may have disappeared there is one possible source of information you can try if you know the area a CO was from and (roughly) the date of their tribunal. There do not appear to have been reporting restrictions on the tribunals so, though they don't seem to have been reported in such national newspapers as *The Times*, there are frequently accounts in the local and regional press. Being newspapers one suspects that there was, even then, a tendency to report all the more sensational cases, hence the headline '"HEIL HITLER" SAYS OBJECTOR' for a story reported in the *Swindon Evening Advertiser* from the Bristol tribunal in July 1940. On the other hand, without a detailed list of individual tribunals, the local press may be your only option. Certainly the *Swindon Evening Advertiser* reported tribunals regularly and in some detail. A report dated 15 June 1940 contains both quotes from one Objector, Bertram Philip Hobbs, of Woodcote near Cirencester, the questions asked of him and the judgement made. Hobbs, a tailor and outfitter, explained: 'My life has been lived in the shadow of the Great War; my earliest recollections are of anxiety felt for my wounded father, and this anxiety has not decreased as the years have passed . . . I believe that war is the result of sin which lies eradicably in the nature of man and of nations.' Questioned by the chairman of the tribunal, Judge Wethered, Hobbs explained that he had devoted his life to fitting himself for the task of spreading knowledge of the Gospel, either by entering the ministry or becoming a missionary. Despite an objection from Hobbs that if they sent him to work on the land it might interfere with his ambition to become a missionary, the tribunal granted him a conditional exemption which required him to be engage in some kind of work on the land, in agriculture, horticulture, forestry or land reclamation.

TNA has numerous files on Conscientious Objectors but most are high-level policy records, though LAB 45/75–LAB 45/77 are handwritten ledgers of the names of some 8,000 applicants for Conscientious Objector status. They are roughly chronological and alphabetical and the contents suggests possibly it was a register drawn up by one of the London tribunals as cases are occasionally shown as being transferred to regional ones.

The Peace Pledge Union, formed in 1934, campaigned actively against the war and in favour of Conscientious Objectors – to the point that MI5 carried out a series of investigations into it, raiding its activists and occasionally prosecuting them. The Peace Pledge Union Archive (see http://www.ppu .org.uk/archives) contains pamphlets and broadsheets of the Central Board for Conscientious Objectors and personal papers of individual COs, including tribunal statements, letters from custody and memoirs of experiences.

## Internees

In September 1939 some 80,000 Germans or Austrians lived in Britain, people who might be considered potential spies or Nazi sympathisers. The Security Service, MI5, advised the Home Office to intern them all and had plans for their detention in special camps belonging to the War Office. The Home Office overruled MI5, initially detaining the 600 aliens considered most dangerous (Category A) and placing movement restrictions on another 6,500 (Category B). The remainder (Category C) were obliged to register with the police (as were all foreigners) but were otherwise left unmolested.

At the time of the Dunkirk evacuations, in a wave of spy mania, thousands of Germans and Austrians, ironically including many Jewish refugees fleeing the Nazis, were rounded up and sent to temporary camps. Even though Italy had not entered the war at this stage many thousands of Italians were also interned. As the invasion threat faded public opinion became more sympathetic to the plight of many individuals and tribunals reviewed their cases and released the majority (though they remained under restrictions, including having to report regularly to the police). The remainder, including many genuine refugees but about whom there were suspicions, were sent to camps on the Isle of Man. Life there was basic but the internees formed educational classes as well as discussion, musical and artistic groups. Their mail was censored, but visitors were permitted and some men were even joined by their families. As the war progressed internees were gradually released – very few were left by 1945.

TNA's HO 396 series contains index card records of mostly Germans, Austrians, Italians and their spouses who were interned or considered for internment during the Second World War. The records are generally alphabetical, though under a number of categories, the main one being 'Internees at Liberty within the UK' (HO 396/1–HO 396/106). Other categories include 'Canada Internees', 'Non Resident Seamen', 'Australian Internees', 'German Internees Released in the UK', 'Italian Internees Released in the UK', a 'Dead Index', 'Germans Interned in UK in 1939' and 'Italians Interned in UK in 1939'. There are various other smaller categories, including people who were repatriated, detainees released in Canada and Australia, detainees abroad returned to Britain and some lists of detainees sent abroad.

Searching for details of an individual can be complex and involve having to look at more than one category, as they may have cards relating to their initial internment and then to their subsequent status after release.

Digital images of all of HO 396/1-106 ('Internees at Liberty within the UK') are available on Moving Here at: http://www.movinghere.org.uk.

There are also images of about 1,000 surviving Metropolitan Police Aliens Registration Cards, MEPO 35 series, searchable and downloadable online at

TNA's DocumentsOnline section. Information provided on the cards includes full name, date of birth, date of arrival in Britain, employment history, address, marital status, details of any children and date of naturalisation, with the Home Office reference if applicable. The cards usually include at least one photograph and for most cases there are continuation cards.

## Second World War Internee Index Records

The cards usually provide very basic details of surname, forenames, date and place of birth, nationality, Police Registration Number, address in Britain, normal occupation, present occupation and address of employer and the decision of the tribunal. Sometimes the back of the index card will give some useful and interesting background information. The card for one teenage girl says: 'Came to UK with parents in August 1936. Jewish. Father was a dental surgeon, but was compelled to give up practice on account of Nazi restrictions on Jews. Father has practice now in Hull. Parents – Category 'C' – reside in Hull.' Another reads:

> This alien is a Jewess. She attained 16 years of age on the 11th April 1940, and had not been before a Tribunal. Her parents are in Vienna. Her

*Alien registration card for Lina Maria Louisa Cavaciuti, detained as an enemy alien.*

father was a bank official. She was brought over by the Movement for the Care of Children from Germany and is a guest at the home of Mr and Mrs Shaffer. Mrs Shaffer is the Hon. Secretary of the Cheltenham Committee for Aiding Refuge Children. The child is attending school. The Advisory Committee considered she could be safely exempted from the special restrictions.

Occasionally the back of the card will mention that the police and MI5 had been consulted by the tribunal.

## Suspected Traitors and Other Internees

During the same spy scare many British citizens were also detained without trial under the Defence Regulations. While some were pacifists, the majority – over 1,000 – were or had been members of Sir Oswald Mosley's British Union (of Fascists). Detainees also included members of other extreme right-wing groups such as the Nordic League, the Imperial Fascist League, the Link and the Right Club. Most prominent of the detainees was the Conservative MP Archibald Maule Ramsay who was interned when it was feared that he was going to attack Churchill in the House of Commons by confronting him with evidence he'd obtained of secret discussions with the Americans. Mosley himself and several of his lieutenants were sent to Brixton, while Lady Diana Mosley, among other women, was sent to Holloway. Many others were sent first to Ascot, Huyton or Walton, for example, and several were later transferred to the Isle of Man: the men to Peveril Camp and the women to Port Erin Camp. Life was basic but the internees set up various classes to occupy themselves. Their mail was censored, but visitors were allowed. During the course of the war many, but not all, detainees were released as security conditions improved.

Searching TNA's website reveals fifteen Home Office files on the camp at Peveril and two files on Port Erin Camp. HO 213/247 contains reports from the Camp Commandant on general conditions at Peveril; HO 215/471 contains a roll of Italian prisoners held at the Metropole Camp on the Isle of Man in October 1943 and HO 215/478 contains a roll of the women's camp in November 1943. Searching the HO series using the word 'detained' between 1939 and 1945 brings up 104 references, some of them to prisoners detained for normal criminal reasons but many relating to political detainees such as HO 45/25571 'Detention of suspects in the event of invasion: lists of persons to be detained; the Suspect List'.

Files on many individual detainees have been released, mainly in the Home Office (HO) records, but some also in files released by MI5 (KV series). HO 45/25719 is the file on Richard Fitzgerald Findlay, a member of the Nordic League, the Right Club and the Link, who became camp leader for the prisoners and whose file contains references to several other prisoners whose cases he argued about with the authorities. HO 45/23667 is the file on Fay

Helen Taylor, a famous female racing driver and member of the British Union of Fascists. HO 45/25732 is the file on Thomas Guillaume St Barbe Baker, member of the British Union of Fascists, the Nordic League and the Link, who held religious meetings in the camp in which he proclaimed Hitler to be the new Messiah. KV 2/1219 and KV 2/1220 are MI5's files on Arthur John Schneider, one of Baker's followers. Most detainees were detained under Defence of the Realm Act Regulation 18B – a search using this produces many useful references.

You should be aware that files on men and women detained are frequently very uncomplimentary about their subjects.

An excellent bibliography on internment, published by the Isle of Man government, is available at: http://www.gov.im/MNH/heritage/library/bibliographies/internment.xml.

There's a very useful leaflet on these records at: http://www.nationalarchives.gov.uk/records/research-guides/internees.htm.

## The Land Army

The Land Army was formed in 1939 and sent young women to work on farms throughout the country. Over 80,000 worked on the land between 1939 and 1948, when the Land Army was finally disbanded. Unfortunately for the family historian records for individuals are sparse. The Land Army was controlled by the Ministry of Food, and the individual service records were destroyed long ago. The ministry's card index of names has been preserved and is at TNA and held on microfiche under reference MAF 421.

The card index will give you only very basic information about each woman, her age, address when she enlisted, and her civilian occupation. Occasionally the card will say 'has had experience on the land' or 'can milk and do dairy work', but often the occupation section will just say something like 'domestic servant', 'student' or 'shop assistant'. Usually the women resigned and there is little other information though sometimes a comment might be added 'resigned to join husband' or 'resigned to return to college with a view to obtaining a diploma for instructional post'. Sadly there are no details of which farms the Land Girl may have worked on or the kind of work they might have done. Please bear in mind that not all Land Girl cards seem to have survived.

## 'Bevin Boys' – The Forgotten Conscripts

In 1942, to try and remedy a shortage of manpower in the nation's coal mines, Minister of Labour Ernest Bevin introduced conscription into the mines. Every month two digits were drawn from a hat and every man whose National Service Registration number ended in one of them was sent down the pits. Only a very few men who had been selected for highly specialised military service were exempted. Some 22,000 men were drawn by ballot and a further 23,000 were allowed to serve in the coal industry voluntarily. Most worked long, hard hours at the coalface after a six-week training period. There were no medals for the 'Bevin Boys' and many men were unjustly criticised for not being in the armed services. The scheme gradually wound down after the war. Famous 'Bevin Boys' included Sir Jimmy Savile OBE, comedian Eric Morecambe and Sir Brian Rix.

Most of the official records for the scheme were destroyed many years ago, including any lists of the men conscripted. There is a description of the working of the ballot system at TNA in LAB 25/196.

## The Channel Islands

In 1940 Britain decided that it could not defend the Channel Islands, outposts very close to the French coast, and their garrisons and Lieutenant Governors were withdrawn. Thousands of British-born inhabitants, and some Channel Islanders, were evacuated to Britain. The first Germans arrived by air and quickly established substantial garrisons on all the islands. Hitler was delighted to have captured part of the British Isles and every opportunity was used for taking propaganda photographs of German soldiers enjoying the Jersey and Guernsey sunshine, talking to policemen and eating ice cream. For the islanders there began nearly five years of occupation, during which time they were forbidden to listen to the BBC, their local press was censored and their movements strictly controlled. The islands were too small to establish an organised resistance group, but many islanders concealed radios to listen secretly to the BBC, helped hide or feed escaped slave labourers (who the Germans brought in to build defences) or did their best to hinder the occupiers. A few succeeded in launching small boats and reaching England. A number of British-born, and a few Channel Islanders, were deported to concentration camps as Hitler considered them a security threat, or because they were Jewish.

All islanders were compelled to complete Registration Cards in 1941. Each card contains a photograph of the individual along with their name, date of birth and address. Children under 14 were recorded on the back of their father's card. Huge numbers of foreign slave labourers were introduced to build enormous concrete fortifications (most of which still survive) and four concentration camps were established on Alderney to hold many of them. After the invasion of France in June 1944 the islanders hoped for liberation but this was not to come until 9 May 1945, when Royal Navy vessels landed troops on Guernsey and Jersey.

Though a search on 'Channel Islands, Guernsey and Jersey' on TNA's website turns up hundreds of file references, these are almost all files on planning their liberation or on events immediately before, or after, liberation. Records relating to the islands' governments, their populations and the experience of occupation are held by their respective island archives: Jersey Archive, Clarence Road, St Helier, JE2 4JY; tel: 01534 833300 (Reception); fax: 01534 833301; email: archives@jerseyheritagetrust.org Internet.

Island Archives, St Barnabas, Cornet Street, St Peter Port, Guernsey, GY1 1LF; tel: 01481 724512; fax: 01481 715814; email: archives@gov.gg.

The website for the Channel Islands Occupation Society Guernsey Branch is at: http://www.occupied.guernsey.net. The Jersey Branch is at: http://www.ciosjersey.org.uk/Intro1.htm.

*Chapter 11*

# CIVIL DEFENCE

## Second World War Civil Defence Areas

Though coordinated from London, Civil Defence was organised on a regional basis, with Headquarters in major cities.

| Region | Area covered | Headquarters |
|---|---|---|
| 1 | Northern | Newcastle |
| 2 | North Eastern | Leeds |
| 3 | North Midland | Nottingham |
| 4 | Eastern | Cambridge |
| 5 | London | London |
| 6 | Southern | Reading |
| 7 | South Western | Bristol |
| 8 | Wales | Cardiff |
| 9 | Midland | Birmingham |
| 10 | Scotland | Edinburgh |
| 11 | South Eastern | Tunbridge Wells |

Civil Defence included the part-time Auxiliary Fire Service, Air Raid Wardens and Fire Watchers, civilian volunteers whose duties were to advise local people about shelters, report bombs and fires in their area to the police and fire brigade, to check on damage and to assist the public. Fire Watchers could be quite young. Les Bowler was still a pupil when he served as one in a team made up of two students and a member of staff at his school: 'We were shown how to put out fire bombs by the ARP people by throwing sacks full of sand over the bomb to keep the air away. The school had a flat roof with skylights and wooden duck boards on the walkways. The night was divided between the three of us, sleeping in the headmaster's office.'

Though Civil Defence was coordinated by the Home Office it was controlled regionally and organised locally by borough, town or county councils and no central record of volunteers seems to exist. Many records have been donated to local record offices and this is the best place to start searching for information. The Glamorgan Record Office has records and log books of various local control centres covering 1940 to 1944 or 1945. Tyne & Wear Archives hold a variety of records, including Fire Watching rosters for North

Shields and an Air Raid Precautions (ARP) register of personnel for 1939–44 for Sunderland. Westminster's collection includes a register of ARP staff; other London boroughs hold copies of the local ARP magazines. It seems likely that ARP service records have long since been destroyed. If your local record office can't help, try approaching your local council to see if they have any records in storage. Don't forget that a lot of council boundaries have changed since the war and possibly a great deal of material has long since been destroyed.

For particular events, or for possible articles that mention Civil Defence units or individuals, the local newspaper can be an invaluable source. Contemporary reports frequently refer to individuals by name, the old principle of selling newspapers that mentioning someone's name means a likely sale applied during wartime just as it does now. In particular, it could be worth looking at newspapers published shortly after VE Day which might have run features on such people as the local Civil Defence or Home Guard. Some local authorities also published brief histories of Civil Defence in their areas so a trip to the local library might turn something up.

## Air Raids

A total of 60,595 civilians died as a result of enemy action in Britain, the overwhelming majority as a result of air raids. It's possible to find basic information on civilian casualties using the Commonwealth War Graves Commission website which records Second World War civilian deaths, and these can be searched for in the same way as military ones. For air-raid victims it will usually give you the casualty's date of death, their address and their place of death – for example, Elizabeth Armstrong of Liverpool is recorded as: 'of 87 Brasenose Road, Bootle. Widow of John Armstrong. Injured 3 May 1941, at 87 Brasenose Road; died at Walton Hospital, Rice Lane'. It also names the reporting authority, in this case it was the County Borough of Liverpool.

There is a detailed list of references to Civil Defence and war damage during the Second World War on TNA website's 'Your Archives' section at: http://yourarchives.nationalarchives.gov.uk/index.php?title=Civil_Defence _and_War_Damage_During_World_War_2, though this is a very high-level listing of possible sources including Home Office, Ministry of Food, Ministry of Health and Ministry of Home Security files.

### Case Study – Swindon Air Raids

Almost every major British city was 'blitzed' in 1940 and 1941, particularly centres of industry and docks, the raids on London, Glasgow and Coventry being particularly remembered, but Plymouth, Bristol, Liverpool, Portsmouth, Belfast, Glasgow and Newcastle, among many others, were badly hit. When Hitler withdrew much of the Luftwaffe for his attack on Russia in the summer, air raids continued, albeit on a reduced scale.

Following a raid by the RAF on the historic German city of Lubeck in March 1942 the Luftwaffe launched a series of retaliatory attacks on British historic cities; Exeter, Bath, Norwich, York and Canterbury were attacked in what became known as the 'Baedecker Blitz', named after the popular guide book which it was assumed the Germans had used in deciding which cities to attack. In early 1944 the Germans began firing unmanned rocket-powered bombs at the South East of England, the smaller V1s, which could be seen and attacked by aircraft and anti-aircraft guns, and the bigger, supersonic V2s, against which there was no defence. In an attempt to carry the raids further north Manchester was attacked by V1s launched from aircraft over the North Sea coast on one occasion. Though the main targets were cities and industrial and military sites no part of Britain was safe from the occasional nuisance raid or from bombs dropped at random from aircraft that had become lost; coastal towns in particular were 'shot up' by attackers that sneaked under the radar. Only at the very end of the war did raids cease altogether.

On 29 August 1942 a high flying German Ju 86 bomber dropped a single bomb on Swindon, killing or fatally injuring eight people. Though a main centre for the Great Western Railway and home of their engineering works, Swindon had suffered only a few minor raids.

*The Swindon Evening Advertiser* reported the raid the same day, but in keeping with the censorship rules could only refer to 'a south west of England town', though it must have been obvious to many readers that it referred to their town. The newspaper report is surprisingly detailed for anyone trying to research the raid:

> A lone raider flying at a great height swooped down over a south-west of England town this morning and dropped one bomb. It fell in the roadway, causing a crater outside the garden of a bungalow. About three houses on either side of the road were demolished and some fifty others were damaged by blast. The plane then veered off, followed by anti-aircraft fire from our guns. The whole of the damage was in a residential area. Three people are known to be dead and four others are in hospital seriously hurt, and a number of others received superficial injuries. In one house Mr and Mrs Blunt escaped serious injury. At the time Mr Blunt was in bed, having returned from all night shift work. He and his wife have already been bombed out of their home in Clapham, London. Their home is a bungalow, and Mrs Blunt received treatment for cuts on the nose. Across the road the breakfast things were being set out on the table, when the occupants went to their indoor shelter. All the occupants were uninjured. ARP, First Aid and ambulance workers were on the scene within a few minutes of the bomb falling, and worked hard, entering all the houses and giving first aid treatment. The district is fairly new and most of the inhabitants work locally. A public house had its windows blown out by the blast. Within half an hour of the bomb

falling children were playing in their front gardens against the background of their blast wrecked homes.

A 'Stop Press' in the same edition of the newspaper read: 'The casualty list in the south town is six people dead and eight in hospital. The dead are Ronald Smith, Thomas Bint, Fred Bathe, Freda Taylor, Sylvester Barrett and William H Roche.' By Monday the number of dead had risen to nine.

The Debt of Honour website records information about the individual casualties. Thomas Bint's details are: 'Husband of Lydia Bint, of 2 Marsh Farm, Shrivenham Road. Injured at Drove Road; died same day at Victoria Hospital.' Fred Bathe, also killed in the blast, 'was Deputy Leader, Rescue Service. Son of Georgina and Thomas Bathe, of High Street, Wroughton; husband of Edith Bathe, of 257 Ferndale Road. Injured at Drove Road; died same day at Victoria Hospital.'

The raid has been analysed, and reported on, along with other raids on Swindon, by a local historian, Mr K Walter, in his paper 'Swindon Air Raids in World War 2 – A review of the remaining evidence', copies of which are available in Swindon Central Library.

Local newspapers can be an excellent source of information on air raids – but not at the time they occurred. For obvious reasons (including the fact that the Germans sometimes didn't actually know exactly where they'd been bombing), reports were kept vague – the *Swindon Evening Advertiser* was obliged to report one raid, on Swindon itself, as 'in a West Country town'. After the war, however, particularly on significant anniversaries, the local paper would often run a feature in which contemporary photographs would be published, along with interviews with survivors, details of damage and casualties and stories from rescue services and witnesses. Given that so many of these people have since died these reports are an invaluable personal resource.

You may also find that local raids have already been researched and written up so a check with your local library or record office might prove productive. Local history groups may also have information or have members who have been researching this topic.

## The Police

During the Second World War the police forces of Britain (of which there were many more than at present, with many boroughs having their own police as well as the county forces) were called upon to carry out many duties in addition to their normal work of keeping the peace and apprehending criminals. They worked closely with the Civil Defence authorities, protecting bomb-damaged sites from potential looters, keeping people away from points of danger and directing traffic. They helped guard sensitive sites and were responsible for ensuring everyone had a gas mask. They had been overseeing a loose system of monitoring resident aliens since the First World War, but controls with regard to this were tightened up and they were given the job of monitoring released detainees and their movements. In the event of invasion a large part of the responsibility for evacuating whole areas would have fallen on them.

A simple search on TNA's website using the word 'police' between the years 1939 and 1945 produces in excess of 3,000 records. Almost all of these, on closer analysis, relate to policy matters, many on liaison between police forces and the military authorities or with Civil Defence.

There are some Metropolitan Police personal records at TNA. There are pension registers in MEPO 21 covering men and women who served in the war years and retired with a pension, though to find a record you'll need to know approximately when your relative retired. Records include personal information about the officer, such as his or her date and place of birth, marital status, parents and next of kin, service details and, from 1923, details of spouse (date of birth and place of their marriage).

Police records of other forces are not public records. Those that survive are held either by the appropriate local record office or the force itself. The City of London Police Records Office, 26 Old Jewry, London, EC2R 8OJ possesses registers listing every member of the force since warrant numbers were introduced on 9 April 1832, together with personal files on 95 per cent of officers who have served since that date.

For the former county and borough forces it's probably best to contact their local record office to see what records they might hold. The Wiltshire and Swindon Record Office at Chippenham, for example, has some records for Wiltshire Constabulary for the war years. If the record office doesn't have information they may be able to tell you who to contact. Many police forces also now have museums or archives – Devon and Cornwall Police (who incorporate both Exeter and Plymouth borough forces) have their Heritage and Learning Resource Centre at Okehampton (http://www.policeheritage-centre.co.uk). There are also some history societies concerned with individual police forces – Hampshire Constabulary History Society has a useful website at: http://hampshireconstabularyhistory.org.uk. It includes advice on researching police ancestors and some helpful links.

The Police Roll of Honour Trust website at: http://www.policememorial .org.uk/Home.htm has individual rolls of honour for each police force, including the Second World War years, giving basic details of officers who died in the course of their duties.

## The National Fire Service

At the start of the war fire brigades were very local indeed, with over 1,400 different services covering the country. This made coordination of forces particularly difficult when it came to German air raids on a large scale. In August 1941 the various local brigades were amalgamated with the Auxiliary

Fires Service, the part-time service of the Civil Defence organisation to become the National Fire Service (NFS). At its peak the NFS employed 370,000 people including some 80,000 women, mainly employed on administrative duties.

TNA holds over 300 files on the NFS, mainly in the Home Office (HO) series but these all seem to be policy files and, as far as I know, no lists of personnel or service records exist, at least at national level.

The NFS was wound up in 1948 and control of fire brigades passed back to local authorities at county and borough level. Some records may survive locally in the record office or with the successor fire brigades.

## Hospitals

During the Second World War hospitals and infirmaries were either private charitable institutions or were run by local authorities. Any surviving records for the institutions are likely to be either in the local record office or held by the successor National Health Trusts. The Hospital Records Database, a joint project of the Wellcome Trust and TNA, contains details of surviving hospital records and can be accessed at: http://www.nationalarchives.gov.uk/hospitalrecords. You can search the databse by the name of the individual hospital or by the town it was in. The website will confirm the types of record that survive and where they are located. Surviving records may, in some cases, contain information on individuals.

For individual nurses some records survive, as a degree of centralisation had begun after the First World War. The General Nursing Council maintained the Register of Nurses (in TNA series DT 10) and the Roll of Nurses (for assistant nurses), which was created in 1944 (in DT 11). The Register and the Roll both contain information of use to family historians including: full name, qualifications, where the individual trained and home address. Any changes to these details may also be recorded, such as change of name upon marriage, change of address, date of death and any removals from the Register of Roll on disciplinary or other grounds.

## Civilian Medals

The Defence Medal was awardable to civilians including members of the Home Guard, Royal Observer Corps, fire brigades, including the National Fire Service, Civil Defence, Messenger Service, police and Coast Guard.

### Gallantry Medals

The senior gallantry award for civilians is the George Cross and there is a useful database of recipients at: http://www.gc-database.co.uk. Other medals included the George Medal and there were specialist medals for the police and other services.

*The London Gazette* is, at least in theory, the best place to start looking for records of civilian awards and a search of *The Times* online may also be useful. If you know roughly when an award was made then once again the local newspaper is a good source as often recipients of awards were, at least for a short time, local celebrities and there will almost certainly be a mention.

HO 250 series are the Minutes and Recommendations of the Inter Departmental Committee on Civil Defence Gallantry Awards. They are arranged chronologically but there is no index available at TNA. If you can find the award in the *London Gazette* this will at least give you a starting point so by dipping into the files and locating the date in the minutes you can, at least in theory, work backwards to the original award.

There are a large number of Civil Defence Organisation medal awards listed in HO 207 series.

Most of the awards are listed by Civil Defence region so a search using key words such as 'Region AND award' or 'Region AND 5 (the Regional Number)' may help you find the award you're looking for. From the catalogue descriptions these all appear to be awards gazetted in the New Year's Honours Lists so checking the *London Gazette* should produce a result.

## AIR 2 Records

Tucked away in the AIR 2 files are a series of files relating to the Civilian Gallantry Awards Committee and its recommendations for medals or other gallantry awards. Though they are in Air Ministry records, they include recommendations for awards to civilians by the Army and Navy (whose copies of the committee records do not seem to have survived). Though the awards are recorded more or less chronologically there are frequently several files covering one year so a search can be difficult. A professional researcher, Paul Baillie, has indexed all the recommendations within AIR 2. He can be contacted via email at: paulbaillie@tiscali.co.uk. For a very reasonable fee he can check his index and provide you with a copy of any surviving recommendation.

## Police Awards

Medals awarded to the police are listed in HO 45 series, but this is a huge series covering just about every aspect of the Home Office's activities. You can trace the lists of awards by searching under 'police AND honours' between the years 1939 and 1945 within HO 45 itself. This search should produce a series of files such as: HO 45/19323 'HONOURS: King's Police Medal: King's Police Medal: list of awards 1943'. These medals will be listed in the *London Gazette* so a search using an individual's name may produce a result.

Policemen who received the King's Police Medal for gallantry are listed in *Police Gallantry 1908–1978* by J Peter Farmery (Periter and Associates, Sydney,

1995), which contains personal details of the recipient, photographs and the original HO 45 reference.

## Fire Brigade Awards

There is a Register of Fire Service Awards, covering the whole country between 1940 and 1970 in HO 187/1838. The Register is indexed by name and each reference includes the full name of the recipient, their rank, their brigade, the date it appeared in the *London Gazette* and, where available, the full citation.

## Railway Awards

The railway companies created their own register of awards for the Second World War, which passed to the government on nationalisation. RAIL 390/1208 'Awards to Railwaymen for Gallantry' covers the years 1941–4. There is more detailed correspondence relating to awards between RAIL 1172/2318 and RAIL 1172/2322, with individual recommendations in RAIL 1172/2323.

## Treasury Records

The Treasury Ceremonial Branch records contain files on the nominations of Civil Defence, police, National Fire Service, Red Cross, Young Men's Christian Association and other personnel for awards with descriptions of the actions warranting recognition. Most of the information in the files was published in supplements to the *London Gazette*, but the files also contain unpublished descriptions of some of the actions leading to nominations for commendations. The papers can relate to actions dating from months earlier. On some files, particularly the later ones, there are papers unconnected in any way with Civil Defence, for example, on awards to civilians who assisted the Allied war effort in occupied countries and following their liberation.

The records are in T336 series, arranged chronologically by the date they appeared in the *London Gazette* so if you can find mention in a particular *Gazette* you can then find the relevant file which will hopefully contain more detailed information.

In the case of all civilian awards it's always worth checking through the local newspaper on, or shortly after, the *Gazette* date as a local award will almost certainly be covered; not only is it likely to give details of the events leading up to the award, it will almost certainly provide leads that will take you back to any original coverage.

## Other Sources for the Home Front

### Local Newspapers

An invaluable source for information on people and events are local newspapers. Though censored, in as much as reports on, for example, air raids do not often name the place being described, they often contain brief articles on the Home Guard, Civil Defence and local servicemen. The *Swindon Evening Advertiser*, for example, in just a couple of issues refers to a local airman, Robert McCarthy, who was awarded the Distinguished Flying Medal for displaying: 'exceptional gallantry and devotion to duty when badly wounded in the legs and stomach during a bombing raid on enemy columns between Echternach and Luxembourg. He continued to operate his radio apparatus until he landed and showed the greatest fortitude while being helped from the rear of the aircraft.' A few days later the paper reports that Platoon Sergeant Major Vernon Thompson of the Oxfordshire and Buckinghamshire Light Infantry had been reported missing in France. A check on the Commonwealth War Graves Commission website doesn't say that he died so presumably Vernon had been taken prisoner.

Contemporary newspapers may provide some information but it's also worth checking them for anniversaries of particular events – things that couldn't be said during the war for censorship reasons may well have been written about after the event, or features written about 'Our Gallant Home Guard' which will contain reminiscences of events from people who are long-since dead.

Local newspapers are usually available through your local library or record office, though if you require a paper from elsewhere you may need to visit the British Library Newspaper Library at Colindale in north London which contains copies of every national newspaper and most British provincial newspapers covering the war years. There is a catalogue of available newspapers that you can use to find local papers available through the British Library Integrated Catalogue at the British Library website at: http://www.bl.uk. Please note that some newspapers may have to be ordered from offsite – also that at some point the British Library is moving its entire collection to digital format where they should be available at the main British Library building near St Pancras.

### Local History Groups or Associations

Though the popularity of local history research has been, perhaps, a little eclipsed in the last few years by the rise in family history these groups continue to be strong and to have a wealth of local knowledge. Members are generally very friendly and interesting and happy to share their knowledge, some of it gleaned after many years of research. Many produce their own

114

publications and have meetings with speakers. Your local library will usually have details and a check on the Internet will usually locate any group interested in the same locality.

There's a useful leaflet on TNA sources for the Home Front at: http://www.nationalarchives.gov.uk/records/research-guides/home-front-1939-1945.htm.

*Chapter 12*

# COMMONWEALTH AND EMPIRE

The British Empire and Commonwealth covered one-quarter of the world's surface in 1939. The Dominions of Canada, Australia, South Africa and New Zealand, which had their own parliaments, declared war almost immediately Great Britain did and sent forces to her assistance. The Indian Empire (consisting of what are now India, Pakistan and Bangladesh) had their own semi-autonomous government under the Viceroy and their own Indian Army, Navy and Air Force, which were also committed to the war. The smaller colonies were effectively ruled from London and their local forces came under the command of British forces in their area and fought alongside them.

When former Commonwealth countries gained independence from Britain, their governments assumed full responsibility for all those who served in the armed forces prior to independence. With the exception of Indian Army officers' records and some Commonwealth servicemen who were in the RAF, all service records were given over to and are now administered and archived by those governments.

## Casualties

The Commonwealth War Graves Commission Debt of Honour website records details of all Empire and Commonwealth casualties and you can search generally under their name or more specifically under the forces of each of the Dominions. Indian troops are recorded generally and there is no specific search facility for them.

A typical record will give the following kind of information:

| | |
|---|---|
| Name | SINGH RAM |
| Nationality | Indian |
| Rank | Lance Naik |
| Regiment | 19th Hyderabad Regiment |
| Unit | 4th Bn |
| Date of Death | 15/02/1942 |
| Service No. | 13279 |

| Additional Information | Son of Hardev Singh, of Kolanaki Dhani, Gurgaon, India |
| Casualty Type | Commonwealth War Dead |
| Grave/Memorial Ref. | Column 304 |
| Memorial | Singapore Memorial |

Most countries have their own rolls of honour, some of which are available online.

## Operational Records

Because Empire and Commonwealth units usually fought under British command copies of their operational records are frequently held alongside the British ones at TNA in Kew, though this is not always the case. It's certainly worth it, if researching in Britain, checking TNA's search engine for any references. WO 179 series contains war diaries from Canadian, South African, New Zealand and Indian Forces. Where possible I've detailed where to find operational records for each country in the relevant section below.

### *Canada*

Over 1,159,000 men and women served in the Canadian Armed Forces during the Second World War (1939–45); 44,093 lost their lives. Canadian forces fought in Western Europe (Canadian troops landed in the disastrous Commando raid at Dieppe in 1942 and 3rd Canadian Division captured Gold Beach at D-Day), Sicily and Italy. Number 6 Group RAF, a Bomber Group, consisted entirely of Canadians. Canadian warships helped protect the vital convoys across the Atlantic.

**Casualties**

The Books of Remembrance contain the names of Canadians who fought in wars and died either during or after them. Online versions of the Second World War books are on the Canadian National Archive site at: http://www.vac-acc.gc.ca/remembers/sub.cfm?source=collections/books/bww2. There is also a searchable database of war graves of Canadians at: http://www.vac-acc.gc.ca/remembers/sub.cfm?source=collections/virtualmem.

**Service Records**

Canadian service records for the Second World War are held at the Library and Archives of Canada and details can be found at: http://www.collection-scanada.gc.ca/genealogy/022-909.007-e.html. Records for Canadian servicemen and women who died during the Second World War are auto-matically open and there is a searchable database at: http://www.collectionscanada.gc.ca/databases/war-dead/index-e.html. If you can identify an individual, you can order either a copy of their entire file or a 'Genealogy Package' which contains selected documents including details of units served in. Requests can be made using an online request form or by writing of faxing to: ATIP and Personnel Records Division, Library and Archives Canada, 395 Wellington Street, Ottawa ON, K1A 0N4; fax: (613) 947 8456.

There are restrictions on release of service records for service personnel who survived the war. There are no restrictions if the individual has been dead for twenty years or more, but it is up to you to provide proof of death. If the individual has been dead for less than twenty years then limited information will be released to immediate family, but it is up to you to provide proof of death and proof of relationship. Requests need to be in writing by either fax or mail to the address above.

More information on the records, proofs of relationship and death and how to apply for copies is available at: http://www.collectionscanada .gc.ca/genealogy/022-909.007-e.html.

### Operational Records

The Library and Archives of Canada contain copies of Army war diaries, ship's logs and Canadian Royal Air Force Operation Records Books, though their website is more difficult to navigate and explore than that of the British TNA.

Copies of war diaries for Canadian Army units are held at Kew in WO 179 series between WO 179/1 and WO179/711 and between WO 179/980 and WO 179/5853. Copies of Operation Record Books for Canadian squadrons serving with the RAF are also at TNA in AIR 27 series.

The website devoted to the Canadian Army in the Second World War is at: http://www.mapleleafup.org; it contains much information and some very sage advice about how to conduct research, especially if using the Internet. It also has a very useful set of links to other Canada-based websites.


## Australia

Almost 1 million Australians served in the Second World War and over 50,000 were killed or wounded. Initially Australian forces were sent to the Mediterranean and Middle East and they fought in Egypt, Libya, Greece and Crete, making a significant contribution to the fighting. After Pearl Harbor was attacked and Japan entered the war on 7 December 1941 Australia's focus naturally shifted to her own defence and the war in the Far East with heavy fighting at Singapore, in the Dutch East Indies and then the advance to the Philippines. Many Australian airmen served with the RAF in both Fighter and Bomber Commands during the course of the war.

### Service Records

A good place to start for Australian service records is the Australian World War 2 Nominal Roll, at: http://www.ww2roll.gov.au, which gives very basic details of over 1 million Australian servicemen and women. You can search for service-record details by specifying any one of name, service number, honours or place (of birth, of enlistment or residential locality at enlistment). Once you find an individual service record you can print a certificate, which provides very basic details of their service, including place and date of enlistment, their service (Air Force, Army or Navy), service number, next of kin, rank, any honours or gallantry awards won and place of discharge. What you won't get are details of their postings and individual units served.

The National Archives of Australia (http://www.naa.gov.au/index.aspx) hold the Second World War service records and it is possible to request a copy of the full service record, which can be viewed online or posted to you as a hard copy, at a cost. If someone has already requested a digital copy then you will find it is already available to be viewed online, at no cost. There is a link directly to the relevant pages of the National Archives of Australia website from the Australian World War 2 Nominal Roll website. The Archive also has an extensive series of fact sheets on the Second World War, available at: http://www.naa.gov.au/about-us/publications/fact-sheets/on-defence/index.aspx#section4.

The Australian War Memorial (http://www.awm.gov.au), their equivalent of our Imperial War Museum, has the Australian Official History of the Second World War online, a searchable roll of honour and profiles of many Australian units, with details of what they did during the war. There are also many Australian Army war diaries which have been digitised and can be examined at: http://www.awm.gov.au/collection/war_diaries.

For information on Royal Australian Navy ships and actions, with ship histories and base histories, access the Royal Australian Navy website at: http://www.navy.gov.au/Main_Page.

**Medals**

Information about Australian medal entitlements is available from: Defence Honours and Awards, T–1–49, Department of Defence, Canberra ACT 2600; tel: 1800 111321; email: honoursandawards@defence.gov.au; website: www.defence.gov.au/medals.

## New Zealand

Though some New Zealand troops were sent to the defence of Britain after the fall of France in 1940 their main contribution was in the Middle East and Western Desert, including fighting in Greece and Crete, then in fierce fighting as part of the 8th Army in Egypt, Libya and Tunisia, then up the length of Italy. Some New Zealand Army units took part in the fighting in the Pacific after Japan entered the war, though her main contribution was from her small navy and the RNZAF. Very many RNZAF personnel flew with the RAF in both Fighter and Bomber Commands over Western Europe. Over 200,000 men and women served in her armed forces at home and abroad during the war.

Copies of war diaries for New Zealand Army units are held at Kew in WO 179 series between WO 179/712 and WO 179/765.

### Service Records

Service records for members of the New Zealand Defence Force (as their former Air Force, Navy and Army are now called) who served in the Second World War are held at: NZDF Archives, Personnel Enquiries, Trentham Military Camp, Private Bag 905, Upper Hutt 5140, New Zealand. Their excellent website at: http://www.nzdf.mil.nz/personnel-records/nzdf -archives/default.htm details the kinds of documents that you'll receive, in particular the History Sheet, the New Zealand equivalent of the British Army's Service and Casualty Form, and explains how they should be interpreted. You can download the various forms required to request a relative's service record and there is an explanation of the archives' rules and charges. The website also has lists of commonly used abbreviations in Second World War records of all three New Zealand services and an extensive bibliography of New Zealand forces in the Second World War.

*The Official History of New Zealand in the Second World War 1939–45*, a series of histories prepared under the supervision of the War History Branch of the Department of Internal Affairs, is available online, with search facilities, at: http://www.nzetc.org/projects/wh2/index.html.

Official records of all three New Zealand armed forces for the Second World War are held at Archives New Zealand in Wellington, website at: http://www.archives.govt.nz. There is an extensive guide to their holdings from the Second World War at: http://archives.govt.nz/research/ guides/war#second.

Additional background information on soldiers and military units may be obtainable from the New Zealand National Army Museum, the website of which is at: http://www.armymuseum.co.nz. Their Kippenberger Military Archives and Research Library contains an extensive collection of published and unpublished material.

The New Zealand Navy Museum's website at: http://www.navymuseum.mil.nz has articles on the Navy's part in the Second World War. The Museum holds a unique collection of objects ranging from functional to ceremonial which represent a full range of events and experiences about the Royal New Zealand Navy.

The Air Force Museum of New Zealand website is at: http:// www.airforcemuseum.co.nz. Their archive includes personal collections, manuscripts and ephemera, log books, journals, technical drawings and publications, maps and a research library of over 3,500 books.

## South Africa

Though there was some reluctance on the part of anti-British politicians to enter the war South Africa did so on 4 September 1939 and some 334,000 men served in her armed forces. South African troops played a prominent role in clearing the Italians out of Abyssinia in 1941 and in the Egyptian desert as part of the 8th Army. South African forces helped capture the island of Madagascar in 1942 and some troops fought in Italy in 1943–5. South African airmen fought in the RAF over Western Europe and a large RAF Training Mission instructed many RAF aircrew in South Africa throughout the war.

War Diaries for South African Army units are held at TNA in WO 179 series between WO 179/766 and WO 179/979. There are Operation Record Books for the South African Air Force (including both operational and administrative units) in AIR 54 series.

Service records for South African Second World War personnel are held at the Department of Defence, Documentation Centre, Private Bag X289, Pretoria 0001, Republic of South Africa. The Department of Defence Archives specialises in military history. It houses the official records of the Department of Defence as well as a collection of unique publications, unit-history files, photographs, maps and pamphlets pertaining to the Department of Defence/SANDF and its predecessors dating from 1912. The Personnel Archives and Reserves, which also forms part of the Documentation Centre, houses the personnel records of all former members of the SANDF and its predecessors.

The National Museum of Military History, at 22 Erlswold Road, Saxonworld, Johannesburg, holds an extensive collection and archive relating to South African military history, with a website at: http://www.ditsong.org.za/militaryhistory.htm.

## India

India was ruled semi-autonomously from London by the Indian government under the Viceroy and had its own armed forces (as well as a substantial garrison of British troops). Though many Indian political leaders such as Gandhi opposed Indian participation in the war, and a small number actively sided with Japan and Germany, India provided over 2 million troops (who fought in East and North Africa and Italy, as well as Iraq, Singapore, Hong Kong and Burma) and huge supplies of materiel. It was partly in recognition of this contribution that India became independent after the war.

Many records relating to the Indian forces are held in the old India Office Collection which now forms part of the Asia, Pacific and African Collections at the British Library at St Pancras: Asia, Pacific and Africa Collections Enquiries, The British Library, 96 Euston Road, London, NW1 2DB; tel: 02074 127873; fax: 02074 127641; email: apac-enquiries@bl.uk.

*A Certificate of Honour awarded by the parish of Charlton Kings, Gloucestershire.*

From friends in Charlton Kings

IN GRATITUDE
for the courage of those who
gave up everything and
went out at unknown cost
to themselves in order to
preserve to their Country
HER FREEDOM OF SOUL

The World War
1939-45

A. MERRITT

The *Indian Army List*, available on the open shelves in the British Library Asia, Pacific and Africa Reading Room (as well as in TNA in their Open Reading Room), gives information on British officers (most officers, especially senior ones, were British) and Indian officers, mainly regarding their regiments and qualifications (Indian Army officers were required to speak several languages). There are service records for Indian Army British officers and British NCOs in the India Office Collection in L/MIL/14 series; for Royal India Naval British officers and Petty Officers in L/MIL/16. There are guides to assist researchers into the British in India at: http://www .bl.uk/reshelp/findhelpregion/asia/india/indiaofficerecordsfamilyhistory/ occupations/occupations.html.

As an occasional visitor to these collections, I would recommend getting there early as the room tends to fill up quickly and you need a desk to be able to order documents. Their document request system is also a little eccentric so don't be afraid to ask the staff, who I have always found to be very friendly and keen to help.

Records for the vast majority of Indian soldiers and Indian officers (there was a general policy between the wars to create more Indian officers) aren't at the British Library. Researches suggest that they are still in India and held by their Ministry of Defence. You could try: Adjutant General's Office, Army HQ, West Block No. III, R K Puram, New Delhi 110066, India.

Copies of war diaries for Indian Army units that served in Britain during the Second World War are held at Kew in WO 179 series between WO 179/5879 and WO 179/5930. You will have to search other theatres (such as WO 169, which covers the Middle East, WO 177, the Medical Services, or WO 172, South East Asia) for Indian units that fought in them.

## *Appendix 1*

# ROYAL NAVAL SHORE ESTABLISHMENTS THAT MIGHT APPEAR ON A SERVICE RECORD

Please note that this list covers both land-based establishments and static ships and is far from comprehensive – for example, I've not included many RN establishments created in Germany in 1945, to which many men must have been posted. The most comprehensive guide to RN shore establishments is Lieutenant Commander B Warlow's *Shore Establishments of the Royal Navy* (Maritime Books, 1992).

| Ship | Location | Purpose |
|------|----------|---------|
| *Abastor* | Tilbury | PLUTO Training Base |
| *Abatos* | Southampton | PLUTO Planning HQ |
| *Aberdonian* | Fort William/Dartmouth | Coastal Forces Depot Ship |
| *Aboukir* | Egypt | Naval Base |
| *Adventure* | Normandy | Beach Repair Ship |
| *Aeolus* | Tring, Herts | Balloon Depot |
| *Aerolite* | Brightlingsea | Accommodation Ship |
| *Afrikander** | Simonstown, South Africa | Naval Base |
| *Alastor* | Burnham on Crouch | Store Depot |
| *Albatross* | Nowera, NSW, Australia | Air Station |
| *Aldebaran* | Murmansk, North Russia | Nominal Depot Ship |
| *Alecto* | Rothesay | Depot Ship |
| *Allenby* | Folkestone | Combined Operations Base |
| *Ambrose* | Dundee | Submarine Base (9th Flotilla) |
| *Ambrose II* | Lerwick | Submarine Base |
| *Anderson* | Colombo | RN Barracks and Radio Station |
| *Appledore* | Appledore, Devon | Landing Craft Base |
| *Appledore II* | Ilfracombe, Devon | Combined Operations Base |
| *Arbella* | Boston, Lincs | Combined Operations Base |
| *Ariel* | Warrington | Air Radio & Mechanics Training School |

*There were at least 6 *Afrikanders* (I–VI) in South Africa and West Africa during the Second World War.

| Ship | Location | Purpose |
|------|----------|---------|
| Armadillo | Glenfinnart | Combined Operations Base |
| Assegai | Durban, South Africa | Naval Base |
| Astraea | Lagos | Naval Base |
| Atlantic Isle | Tristan de Cunha | Meteorological Station |
| Attack | Portland | Combined Operations Base |
| Avalon I, II & III | Newfoundland | Accommodation Ships and Accounts Base |
| Bacchante | Station Hotel, Aberdeen | Nominal Depot Ship |
| Badger | Harwich | Flag Officer's Headquarters |
| Baldur | Iceland | Naval Base |
| Baldur II | Reykjavik, Iceland | W/T Station and Transit Camp |
| Baldur III | Hvitanes, Iceland | Naval Base |
| Bambara | Trincomalee, Sri Lanka | Air Station |
| Basilisk | Port Moresby | Naval Base |
| Beaver | Hull | Naval Base |
| Beaver II | Immingham | Naval Base (Tug Depot) |
| Bee | Weymouth | Coastal Forces Base |
| Beehive | Felixstowe | Coastal Forces Base |
| Bellatrix | Murmansk | Nominal Depot Ship |
| Benbow | Trinidad | Naval Base |
| Bherunda | Colombo, Ceylon | Air Station |
| Birnbeck | Weston-super-Mare | Experimental Weapons Station |
| Blackcap | Warrington | Air Station |
| Blazer | Bembridge, Isle of Wight | Gunnery Range |
| Bonaventure | Loch Striven | Submarine Depot Ship |
| Braganza | Bombay | Naval Base |
| Bristol | Bristol | Two Training Establishments |
| Brittania | Dartmouth | Royal Naval College |
| Bull | Massawa, Eritrea | Naval Base |
| Bunting | Harwich | Auxiliary Patrol Base |
| Burong | Mandapam, India | Minesweeper Base |
| Buzzard | Kingston, Jamaica | Air Station |
| Byrsa | Naples | Naval Base |
| Cabbala | Falfield, Glos | Coding School |
| Cabot | Bristol (then Wetherby) | Training Establishment |
| Caledonia | Rosyth | Boys Training Establishment |
| Calliope | Tyneside | Royal Naval Reserve Base |
| Cannae | Bone, Algeria | Nominal Depot Ship |
| Canopus | Alexandria | Training Establishment |
| Caroline | Belfast | Naval Base |
| Caroline II | Belfast | Trawler Base |
| Carrick | Greenock | Training/Accommodation Ship |
| Caserne Bir Hacheim | Emsworth, Hants | Free French Drafting Depot |
| Caserne Birot | Greenock | Free French Shore Base |
| Caserne Surcouf | Clapham Common | Free French Transit Establishment |
| Celebrity | Milford Haven | Trawler Base |
| Centurion | Devonport | Trawler Base Ship/Dummy Battleship |

| Ship | Location | Purpose |
|------|----------|---------|
| Cerberus | Williamstown, Victoria | Royal Australian Navy Base |
| Chaleur | Quebec | Royal Canadian Navy Depot Ship |
| Chembur | Bombay | Royal Marine Camp |
| Chinkara | Cochin | Landing Craft Base |
| Cicala | Dartmouth | Coastal Forces Base |
| Clio | Barrow-in-Furness | Naval Base |
| Cochrane | Rosyth | Naval Base |
| Cockfosters | London | Holding Depot |
| Collingwood | Fareham, Hants | Maritime Warfare School |
| Collingwood II | Southampton | Pay Centre |
| Colonsay | Grimsby | Minesweeper Base |
| Condor | Arbroath | Air Station |
| Coonwara | Darwin | Royal Australian Navy Depot |
| Copra | Largs | Combined Operations Admin Base |
| Cormorant | Gibraltar | Naval Base |
| Cricket | Burlesdon, Hants | Landing Craft Base |
| Daedalus | Lee-on-Solent | Air Station |
| Dartmouth | Dartmouth | Landing Craft Training |
| Defender | Liverpool | Ocean Escort Base |
| Defiance | Devonport | Training Establishment |
| Demetrius | Wetherby | Accounting Base |
| Dinosaur | Troon | Combined Operations Base |
| Dipper | Henstridge, Somerset | Air Station |
| Dolphin | Gosport | Submarine Depot |
| Dorlin | Acharacle, Argyll | Combined Operations Base |
| Dragonfly | Hayling Island | Combined Operations Base |
| Drake | Devonport | Naval Barracks |
| Drake I–V | Devonport | Accounting Bases |
| Dryad | Portsmouth | Navigation School |
| Duke | Great Malvern | Training Establishment |
| Dumana | Alexandria | Depot Ship |
| Dundonald | Auchengate | Combined Operations Signals School |
| Dunluce Castle | Scapa Flow | Accommodation Ship |
| Eaglet | Liverpool | Shore Base |
| Eaglet II | Birkenhead | Anti-Submarine and Minesweeper Base |
| Easton | Rosyth | Harbour Training Ship |
| Effingham | Dartmouth | Combined Operations Base |
| Eland | Freetown, Sierra Leone | Naval Base |
| Elfin | Blyth | Submarine Base |
| Elfin II | Blyth | Coastal Forces Base |
| Elissa | Messina, Sicily | Coastal Operations Base |
| Emerald Star | Fishguard | Experimental Station |
| Emperor of India | Ipswich | Anti-aircraft then Accommodation Ship |
| Epping | Harwich | Minesweeper Base |
| Eridge | Alexandria | Base Ship |
| Euphrates | Basra, Iraq | Depot Ship |

| Ship | Location | Purpose |
|---|---|---|
| *Europa* | Lowestoft | Patrol Service Central Depot |
| *Europa II* | Bungay | Overflow Camp |
| *Excalibur* | Stoke-on-Trent | New Entry Seaman Training Base |
| *Excellent* | Whale Island | Naval Gunnery School |
| *Excellent II* | Portsmouth/Chelsea | Accounting Base |
| *Fann* | Dakar, Senegal | Naval Base |
| *Faraway* | Greenock | HQ Flag Officer, Carrier Training |
| *Fermoy II* | Alexandria | Accounting Base |
| *Ferret* | Londonderry | Naval Base |
| *Fervent* | Ramsgate | Naval Base |
| *Fledgling* | Eccleshall, Staffs | WRNS Air Mechanic Training Camp |
| *Flowerdown* | Flowerdown, Winchester | Radio Station |
| *Flycatcher* | Ludham, Norfolk | Air Station |
| *Flying* Fox | Bristol | Royal Naval Reserve Base |
| *Foliot* | Plymouth | Accommodation Camp |
| *Foliot I–IV* | Plymouth | Landing Craft Bases |
| *Forte* | Falmouth | Naval Base |
| *Fortitude II* | Ardrossan | Coastal Forces Base |
| *Forward* | Newhaven | Naval Base and Intelligence Centre |
| *Forward II* | Newhaven | Coastal Forces Base |
| *Fox* | Lerwick, Shetland | Naval Base |
| *Fox II* | Lerwick, Shetland | Coastal Forces Base |
| *Gadwall* | Belfast | Air Station |
| *Gamunu* | Ceylon | RNVR Base |
| *Ganges* | Harwich | Boys Training Establishment |
| *Gannet I, II* and *II* | Northern Ireland | Air Stations |
| *Garuda* | Coimbatore, India | Aircraft Repair Yard |
| *General Gordon* | Gravesend | Training Establishment |
| *Gipsy* | Swansea | Minesweeping Base |
| *Glendower* | Pwllheli | Seamanship Training Establishment |
| *Godwit* | Ollerton, Salop | Air Station |
| *Goldcrest* | Angle, Pembrokeshire | Air Station |
| *Golden Hind* | Sydney, Australia | Manning Depot |
| *Goldfinch* | Takali, Malta | Air Station |
| *Good Hope* | Port Elizabeth, South Africa | Training Establishment |
| *Goshawk* | Trinidad | Air Station |
| *Gosling* | Risley, Lancs | Fleet Air Arm Training Establishment |
| *Grasshopper* | Weymouth | Coastal Forces Base |
| *Grebe* | Alexandria | Air Station |
| *Gregale* | Malta | Coastal Forces Base |
| *Gunmetal* | Messina, Sicily | Naval Base |
| *Haig* | Rye | Combined Operations Base |
| *Hamilcar* | Algeria/Messina | Landing Craft Base |
| *Hannibal* | Algiers/Taranto | Naval Base |
| *Happy Lass* | Portsmouth | Accommodation Ship for WRNS |
| *Hasdrubal* | Bizerta, Tunisia | Naval Base |
| *Haslar* | Gosport | Naval Hospital |
| *Hathi* | Delhi/Ceylon | Naval Depot |

| Ship | Location | Purpose |
|------|----------|---------|
| *Headingley* | Headingley, Lancs | WRNS Training Establishment |
| *Hecla* | Clyde/Iceland | Destroyer Depot Ship |
| *Helder* | Brightlingsea | Combined Operations Base |
| *Heron* | Yeovilton | Air Station |
| *Hesperides* | Fayal, Azores | Naval Base |
| *Highflyer* | Trincomalee | Naval Base |
| *Hilsa* | Mandapam, India | Coastal Forces Base |
| *Hopetoun* | Port Edgar | Landing Craft/Minesweeping Base |
| *Hornbill* | Culham, Abingdon | Receipt & Despatch Centre |
| *Hornet* | Gosport | Coastal Forces Base |
| *Imperieuse* | Gareloch/Devonport | Training Establishment for Stokers |
| *Impregnable* | Devonport | Boys Training Establishment |
| *Irma* | Scapa Flow | Repair Unit |
| *Ironclad* | Diego Suarez | Naval Base |
| *Iskra* | Gibraltar | Coastal Forces Base |
| *Jackdaw* | Crail, Fife | Air Station |
| *Jufair* | Bahrain | Naval Base |
| *Jules Verne* | Harwich | Depot Ship |
| *Kaluga* | Cochin, India | Air Station |
| *Kedah* | Singapore/Chittagong | Coastal Forces Base |
| *Kestrel* | Worthy Down, Hants | Air Station |
| *Kilele* | Tanga, Tanganyika | Air Station |
| *King Alfred* | Hove | Royal Naval Volunteer Reserve Training |
| *Kipanga* | Kallindini, Kenya | Air Station |
| *Kongoni* | Durban, South Africa | Naval Base |
| *Korongo* | Nairobi, Kenya | Aircraft Repair Yard |
| *Ladbroke* | Syracuse, Sicily | Naval Base |
| *Landguard* | Colombo, Ceylon | Naval Base |
| *Landlock* | Singapore | Mobile Landing Craft Advanced Base |
| *Landrail* | Campbeltown | Air Station |
| *Landswell* | Cochin/Singapore | Mobile Landing Craft Advanced Base |
| *Lanka* | Colombo | Naval Base |
| *Leigh* | Southend-on-Sea | Naval Base |
| *Leonidas* | Takoradi, Gold Coast | Naval Base |
| *Lizard* | Shoreham | Combined Operations Base |
| *Lochinvar* | Port Edgar | Minesweeper Training Base |
| *Macaw* | Wellbank, Cumberland | Transit Camp |
| *Maidstone* | Med/Scapa/Gibraltar | Submarine Depot Ship |
| *Maidstone II* | Alexandria | Accounting Base |
| *Malabar* | Bermuda and Jamaica | Naval Base |
| *Malagas* | Cape Town, South Africa | Air Station |
| *Manatee* | Yarmouth, Isle of Wight | Landing Craft Base |
| *Manela* | Iceland | Accommodation Ship |
| *Mantis* | Lowestoft | Coastal Forces Base |
| *Maraga* | Addu Attoll | Air Station |
| *Marlborough* | Eastbourne | Training Establishment |
| *Martello* | Lowestoft | Auxiliary Patrol Base |

| Ship | Location | Purpose |
|------|----------|---------|
| Martial | Alexandria | Mobile Naval Base Defence Organisation Depot Ship |
| Marve | Bombay | Royal Marine Camp |
| Mashobra | Narvik | Mobile Naval Base Defence Organisation Base Ship (1940) |
| Mastodon | Exbury, Southampton | Combined Operations Base |
| Mayina | Colombo | Transit and Holding Camp |
| Medina | Hyde, Isle of Wight | FAA Camp/Landing Craft Base |
| Medway | Alexandria | Accounting Base |
| Medway II | Beirut/Malta | Submarine Base |
| Melampus | Bathurst, Gambia | Naval Base |
| Menace | Portsmouth | Mobile Naval Base Defence |
| Mentor | Stornoway | Minesweeper Base |
| Mentor II | Stornoway | Coastal Forces Base |
| Mercury | East Meon | Royal Naval Signals School |
| Mercury II | Haslemere | Experimental Signals Establishment |
| Merganser | Crimond | Air Station |
| Merlin | Donibristle | Air Station |
| Mersey | Liverpool | Depot |
| Midge | Great Yarmouth | Coastal Forces Base |
| Minos | Lowestoft | Naval Base |
| Minos II | Lowestoft | Coastal Forces Base |
| Miranda | Great Yarmouth | Minesweeper Base |
| Mirtle | Secret Location | Mine Investigation Range |
| Moira | Freetown | Base and Accommodation Ship |
| Monara | Maharagama, Ceylon | Aircraft Repair Yard |
| Monck | Port Glasgow | Landing Craft Base |
| Monck II | Greenock | HQ Flag Officer |
| Monster | Fortrose, Inverness | Combined Operations Base |
| Moreta | Haifa | Naval Base |
| Morgan | Kingston, Jamaica | Naval Base |
| Mosquito | Alexandria | Coastal Forces Base |
| Mosquito I, II, II | Eastern Mediterranean | Coastal Forces Bases |
| Nasar | Sembawang | Air Station |
| Nelson | Portsmouth | Royal Naval Barracks |
| Nemo | Brightlingsea | Auxiliary Patrol Base |
| Neptune | Faslane | Submarine Base |
| Newfoundland | Devonport | Training Ship |
| Newt | Newhaven | Combined Operations Base |
| Nightjar | Inskip, Lancs | Air Station |
| Nile | Alexandria | Naval Base |
| Nimrod | Campbeltown | Training Establishment |
| Northman | Faroes | Naval Base |
| Northney | Hayling Island | Landing Craft Base |
| Nuthatch | Anthorn, Cumberland | Air Station |
| Odyssey | Ilfracombe/London | Naval Accounting Base |
| Orlando | Greenock | Naval Base |
| Osborne | Isle of Wight | Naval Base |

| Ship | Location | Purpose |
|------|----------|---------|
| *Osprey* | Portland/Dunoon, Northern Ireland | Naval Base |
| *Owl* | Fearn, Ross-shire | Air Station |
| *Paragon* | Hartlepool | Minesweeping Base |
| *Pasco* | Glenbranter | Landing Craft Signal School |
| *Pauline* | Lymington, Hants | Combined Operations Base |
| *Peewit* | East Haven, Angus | Air Station |
| *Pembroke* | Chatham | Royal Naval Barracks |
| *Pembroke II* | Chatham | Accounting Base |
| *Pembroke III* | London | WRNS Accounting Base |
| *Pembroke IV* | The Nore | Accounting Base |
| *Pembroke V* | Dover/London | Secret Base |
| *Pembroke X* | Lowestoft | RN Patrol Service Base |
| *Peregrine* | Ford, Sussex | Air Station |
| *Pharos* | Alexandria | Torpedo School |
| *Philoctetes* | Freetown | Depot Ship |
| *Philoctetes II, III* | Freetown | Accounting Bases |
| *Phoenicia* | Manoel Island, Malta | Naval Accounting Base |
| *Phoenix* | Egypt | Aircraft Repair Yard |
| *Pigmy* | Gibraltar | Submarine Base |
| *Pleaides* | Scapa Flow | Trawler Base |
| *Polar Bear* | Thorshavn, Faroes | Naval Base |
| *Pomona* | Scapa Flow | Boom Defence Depot |
| *Porcupine* | Portsmouth | Landing Craft/Minesweeper Base |
| *Porcupine II* | Portsmouth | Combined Operations Base |
| *President I–VI* | London | Naval Accounting Bases |
| *Prometheus* | Alexandria | Auxiliary Patrol Base |
| *Prosperine* | Lyness, Scapa Flow | Naval Base |
| *Providence* | Ramsgate | Auxiliary Patrol Base |
| *Purbeck* | Weymouth | Landing Craft Base |
| *Pursuivant* | Falkland Islands | Naval Base |
| *Pyramus* | Orkney | Minesweeping Base |
| *Pyramus II* | Kirkwall | Northern Patrol Trawler Base |
| *Quebec* | Inverary | Combined Operations Training Base |
| *Quebec II* | Inverary | Combined Operations Training Centre |
| *Racer* | Larne | Minesweeper & Anti-submarine Base |
| *Racer II* | Larne | Coastal Forces Base |
| *Ragea* | Alexandria | Coastal Forces Base |
| *Rajaliya* | Puttalam, Ceylon | Air Station |
| *Raleigh* | Torpoint, Cornwall | Royal Naval Training Establishment |
| *Rapax* | Hiswa, Aden | Air Station |
| *Raven* | Eastleigh | Air Station |
| *Razorbill* | Algiers | Coastal Forces Base |
| *Reliable* | Falmouth | Landing Craft Servicing |
| *Rigorous* | Grimsby | Naval Base |
| *Ringtail* | Burscough, Lancs | Air Station |
| *Ringtail II* | Woodvale, Lancs | Air Station |

| Ship | Location | Purpose |
|------|----------|---------|
| *Robertson* | Sandwich, Kent | Landing Craft Base |
| *Robin* | Kirkwall, Orkneys | Air Station |
| *Rodent* | Coldhayes, Hants | Special Boat Unit HQ |
| *Romola* | Lowestoft | Minesweeping Base |
| *Rooke* | Rosyth | Boom Defence Depot |
| *Roseneath* | Roseneath | Combined Operations Base |
| *Royal Albert* | London and Germany | Naval Accounting Base |
| *Royal Arthur* | Skegness | Training Establishment |
| *Royal Charter* | Grimsby | Auxiliary Patrol Base |
| *St Angelo* | Malta | Naval Base/Accounting Base |
| *St Barbara* | Bognor Regis | Anti-aircraft Range |
| *St Bedes* | Eastbourne | Wireless School |
| *St Christopher* | Fort William | Combined Operations Training Base |
| *St Clement* | Tilbury | Combined Operations Base |
| *St Elmo* | Swansea | Base Accountants Office |
| *St George* | Isle of Man | Royal Naval Training Establishment |
| *St George* | Portsmouth | Gunnery Range (Eastney) |
| *St Helier* | Dartmouth | Landing Craft Base |
| *St Mathew* | Burnham-on-Crouch | Combined Operations Training Base |
| *St Vincent* | Gosport | Royal Naval Training Establishment |
| *Saker* | New York, USA | Naval Accounting Base |
| *Salcombe* | Exmouth | Combined Operations Base |
| *Salsette* | Bombay | Combined Operations Base |
| *Sambur* | Mauritius | Air Station |
| *Sanderling* | Abbotsinch | Air Station |
| *Sandfly* | Peterhead | Coastal Forces Base |
| *Sangdragon* | Seychelles | Naval Base |
| *Saunders* | Kabrit, Egypt | Combined Operations Training Base |
| *Scipio* | Oran | Naval Base |
| *Scotia* | Doonfoot/Warrington | Signals Training Establishment |
| *Sea Eagle* | Londonderry | Naval Base |
| *Seahawk* | Culdrose | Air Station |
| *Sea Serpent* | Chichester | Landing Craft Base |
| *Sheba* | Aden | Naval Base |
| *Shrapnel* | Southampton | Naval Base |
| *Shrapnel II* | Southampton | Stokers Training Establishment |
| *Shrike* | Maydown, Northern Island | Air Station |
| *Simbang* | Sembawang, Singapore | Air Station and Royal Marine Camp |
| *Skirmisher* | Milford Haven | Naval Base |
| *Skirmisher II* | Pembroke Dock | Coastal Forces Base |
| *Somers Isles* | Bermuda | Working Up Base |
| *Sparrowhawk* | Orkneys | Air Station |
| *Spartiate* | Glasgow | Base Depot Ship |
| *Spartiate II* | Tullichewan | WRNS Training Establishment |
| *Sphinx* | Alexandria | Naval Accommodation Camp |
| *Spurwing* | Sierra Leone | Air Station |
| *Squid* | Southampton | Landing Craft Base |
| *Stag* | Port Said | Naval Base |

| Ship | Location | Purpose |
|------|----------|---------|
| *Standard* | Kielder, Northumberland | Rehabilitation Centre (Psychiatric) |
| *Stopford* | Bo'ness, West Lothian | Combined Operations Training Base |
| *Sultan* | Singapore | Naval Base/Accounting Base |
| *Sutor* | Cromarty | Landing Craft Base |
| *Tadpole* | Poole | Coastal Forces Base |
| *Tagarin* | Freetown, Sierra Leone | Naval Base |
| *Tamar* | Hong Kong | Naval Base |
| *Tana* | Kilindini, Kenya | Naval Base |
| *Tawe* | Swansea | Auxiliary Patrol Base |
| *Temeraire* | Portsmouth | Naval Physical Training School |
| *Tengra* | Mandapam, India | Combined Operations Base |
| *Tern* | Twatt, Orkney | Air Station |
| *Terror* | Singapore | Naval Base |
| *Thunderer* | Keyham, Plymouth | Naval Engineering School |
| *Torch* | Holyhead | Minesweeper/Coastal Forces Base |
| *Tormentor* | Hamble, Southampton | Combined Operations Base |
| *Trelawney* | Loch Alsh | Secret Minelaying Base |
| *Triphibian* | Lytham St Annes | Training Establishment |
| *Tullichewan* | Ballock | Combined Operations Base |
| *Tunsberg* | Liverpool | Norwegian Naval Depot |
| *Turnstone* | Watford | Air Fitters Training Establishment |
| *Turtle* | Poole | Landing Craft Base |
| *Ukussa* | Ceylon | Air Station |
| *Urley* | Isle of Man | Air Station |
| *Valkyrie* | Douglas, Isle of Man | RN Radar Training Establishment |
| *Valkyrie II* | Douglas, Isle of Man | Training Establishment |
| *Valkyrie IV* | Douglas, Isle of Man | Training Establishment |
| *Valluru* | Madras, India | Air Station |
| *Varbel* | Port Bannatyne | Midget Submarine Base |
| *Varbel II* | Loch Striven | Midget Submarine Base |
| *Vernon* | Portsmouth | Royal Naval Training Establishment |
| *Victory* | Portsmouth | Naval Accounting Base |
| *Victory I, II* | Goodings, Newbury | Naval Accounting Section |
| *Victory III, IV* | Portsmouth | Naval Accounting Section |
| *Victory V* | Portsmouth | Combined Headquarters |
| *Volcano* | Holmbrook, Cumberland | Bomb Disposal Training Base |
| *Vulture* | St Merryn | Air Station |
| *Vulture II* | Treligga | Bombing & Gunnery Range |
| *Wagtail* | Heathfield, Ayr | Air Station |
| *Wara* | Gold Coast | Air Station |
| *Warren* | Largs | Combined Operations Base |
| *Wasp* | Dover | Coastal Forces Base |
| *Watchful* | Great Yarmouth | Anti-submarine/Minesweeper Base |
| *Waxwing* | Dunfermline | Accommodation Camp |
| *Wellesley* | Liverpool | Training Establishment |
| *Wessex* | Southampton | Royal Naval Reserve Base |
| *Westcliffe* | Southend | Landing Craft Base |
| *Western Isles* | Tobermory | Working Up Base |

| Ship | Location | Purpose |
|------|----------|---------|
| *Wildfire* | Gillingham | Combined Operations/Accounting Base |
| *Woolverstone* | Ipswich | Landing Craft Base |
| *Yeoman* | Thames | Naval Base |

Please note that Naval Accounting Bases are usually nominal postings and that the person in question is likely to be serving elsewhere, just paid through the Accounting Base. This should be clear on the service record which will say something like '*Victory* – for service with Naval Intelligence Division' or '*Saker* – for service with British Naval Mission to USA'. Some Accounting Bases have more than one reference, i.e. *Victory II*, because rapid growth in the Navy meant some Accounting Bases had to be split up for ease of administration.

# ARMY ABBREVIATIONS – UNITS

| | |
|---|---|
| AAC | Army Air Corps |
| AARR | Airborne Armoured Reconnaissance Regiment |
| ACC | Army Catering Corps |
| ACD | Army Chaplains Department |
| ADS | Army Dental Service |
| AEC | Army Education Corps |
| AHC | Army Hospital Corps |
| ALS | Army Legal Services |
| APC | Army Pay Corps |
| A&SH | Argyl & Sutherland Highlander |
| AVC | Army Veterinary Corps |
| AYR YEO | Ayrshire Yeomanry |
| BEDF R | Bedfordshire Regiment |
| BEDF YEO | Bedfordshire Yeomanry |
| BORD R | Border Regiment |
| BUCKS YEO | Buckinghamshire Yeomanry |
| BWIR | British West Indies Regiment |
| CAMB R | Cambridgeshire Regiment |
| CAMC | Canadian Army Medical Corps |
| CAMN HIGHS | Cameron Highlanders |
| C GDS | Coldstream Guards |
| CHES R | Cheshire Regiment |
| CHES YEO | Cheshire Yeomanry |
| CL YEO | City of London Yeomanry |
| CMP | Corps of Military Police |
| C OF AS | Corps of Army Schoolmasters |
| C OF LOND YEO | City of London Yeomanry |
| CO OF LOND YEO | County of London Yeomanry |
| CONN RANG | Connaught Rangers |
| DCLI | Duke of Cornwall's Light Infantry (also D OF CORN LI) |
| DENBIGH YEO | Denbighshire Yeomanry |
| DEVON R | Devonshire Regiment |
| DG or D GDS | Dragoon Guards |
| DLI | Durham Light Infantry (also DURH LI) |
| D OF LANCS OY | Duke of Lancaster's Own Yeomanry |
| DORSET R | Dorset Regiment |

| | |
|---|---|
| DORSET YEO | Dorset Yeomanry |
| DTR | Driver Training Regiment |
| ER OF YORK Y | East Riding of Yorkshire Yeomanry |
| ESSEX R | Essex Regiment |
| ESSEX YEO | Essex Yeomanry |
| E SURREY R | East Surrey Regiment |
| E YORK R | East Yorkshire Regiment |
| FANY | First Aid Nursing Yeomanry |
| FF REGT | Frontier Force Regiment (India) |
| GCR | Gold Coast Regiment |
| G GDS | Grenadier Guards |
| GLAM YEO | Glamorgan Yeomanry |
| GLOUC R | Gloucester Regiment |
| GMP | Garrison Military Police |
| GORD HIGHS | Gordon Highlanders (also written as GORDONS) |
| GRKS | Gurkhas |
| HAC | Honourable Artillery Company |
| HAC ART | Honourable Artillery Company Artillery Section |
| HAC INF | Honourable Artillery Company Infantry Section |
| HAMPS R | Hampshire Regiment |
| HAMPS YEO | Hampshire Yeomanry |
| HEREFORD R | Hereford Regiment |
| HERT R | Hertfordshire Regiment (also written as HERTS R) |
| HERTS YEO | Hertfordshire Yeomanry |
| HIGH LI | Highland Light Infantry (also HLI) |
| HRS | Hussars |
| I GDS | Irish Guards (also IR GDS) |
| INT CORPS | Intelligence Corps |
| KAR | Kings African Rifles |
| KORL | Kings Own Royal Lancaster Regiment |
| KOSB | Kings Own Scottish Borderers (also KO SCOT BORD) |
| KOYLI | Kings Own Yorkshire Light Infantry |
| KRRC | Kings Royal Rifle Corps (also KR RIF C) |
| KSLI | Kings Shropshire Light Infantry |
| LABOUR C | Labour Corps (also LC) |
| LANARK YEO | Lanarkshire Yeomanry |
| LAN FUS | Lancashire Fusiliers |
| LCRS | Lancers (also written LRS) |
| LEIC R | Leicestershire Regiment |
| LEIC YEO | Leicestershire Yeomanry |
| LEINS R | Leinster Regiment |
| LG | Life Guards (also L GDS) |
| LINC R | Lincolnshire Regiment |
| LIR | London Irish Rifles |
| L N LAN R | Loyal North Lancashire Regiment |
| LOND R | London Regiment |
| LOTH & BORD H | Lothian & Border Horse |
| LOVAT SCTS | Lovat Scouts |
| L'POOL R | Liverpool Regiment |

| | |
|---|---|
| LRDG | Long Range Desert Group |
| MANCH R | Manchester Regiment |
| MIDDX R | Middlesex Regiment |
| MONMOUTH R | Monmouthshire Regiment |
| MPSC | Military Provost Staff Corps |
| MTF | Mauritius Territorial Force |
| NORF R | Norfolk Regiment |
| NORF YEO | Norfolk Yeomanry |
| NORTHD FUS | Northumberland Fusiliers |
| NORTHD YEO | Northumberland Yeomanry |
| NORTHTN R | Northamptonshire Regiment |
| NORTHTN YEO | Northamptonshire Yeomanry |
| N SOM YEO | North Somerset Yeomanry |
| N STAFF R | North Staffordshire Regiment |
| OBLI | Oxfordshire and Buckinghamshire Light Infantry (also OX & BUCKS LI) |
| OXF YEO | Oxfordshire Yeomanry |
| PARA REGT | Parachute Regiment |
| PEMBROKE YEO | Pembrokeshire Yeomanry |
| PPA | Popski's Private Army (Special Forces in the desert and Italy) |
| QARANC | Queen Alexandra's Royal Army Nursing Corps |
| GLASGOW YEO | Queens Own Royal Glasgow Yeomanry |
| QUEENS SR | Queens Royal West Surrey Regiment (usually just QUEENS) |
| RA | Royal Artillery |
| RAC | Royal Armoured Corps |
| RACHD | Royal Army Chaplains Department |
| RADC | Royal Army Dental Corps |
| RAEC | Royal Army Education Corps |
| RAMC | Royal Army Medical Corps |
| RAOC | Royal Army Ordnance Corps |
| RAPC | Royal Army Pay Corps |
| RASC | Royal Army Service Corps |
| RAVC | Royal Army Veterinary Corps |
| R BERKS R | Royal Berkshire Regiment |
| RC | Reconnaissance Corps |
| RCT | Royal Corps of Transport |
| R DEVON YEO | Royal Devon Yeomanry |
| R D FUS | Royal Dublin Fusiliers (also R DUB FUS) |
| RE | Royal Engineers |
| RE KENT YEO | Royal East Kent Yeomanry |
| RFA | Royal Field Artillery |
| R FUS | Royal Fusiliers |
| RGA | Royal Garrison Artillery |
| RGH | Royal Gloucestershire Hussars |
| R GUERNSEY LI | Royal Guernsey Light Infantry |
| RHA | Royal Horse Artillery |
| RHF | Royal Highland Fusiliers |
| RH GDS | Royal Horse Guards (also appears as RHG) |
| R HIGHRS | Royal Highlanders |

| | |
|---|---|
| RIF | Royal Irish Fusiliers (also appears as R IR FUS) |
| RIF BRIG | Rifle Brigade |
| R INNS FUS | Royal Inniskilling Fusiliers |
| RIR | Royal Irish Rifles |
| R LANC R | Royal Lancaster Regiment |
| RMP | Royal Military Police |
| R MUNS FUS | Royal Munster Fusiliers |
| R N DEVON YEO | Royal North Devon Yeomanry |
| RPC | Royal Pioneer Corps |
| RRF | Royal Regiment of Fusiliers |
| R SCOTS | Royal Scots |
| R S FUS | Royal Scots Fusiliers (also R SC FUS) |
| R SIGS | Royal Signals (also R SIGNALS) |
| RSR | Raiding Support Regiment (Special Forces in Italy and Adriatic) |
| R SUSS R | Royal Sussex Regiment |
| RTR | Royal Tank Regiment |
| RUR | Royal Ulster Rifles |
| R W FUS | Royal Welsh Fusiliers |
| RW KENT R | Royal West Kent Regiment |
| R WAR R | Royal Warwickshire Regiment |
| SAS | Special Air Service |
| SCO H | Scottish Horse |
| SCO RIF | Scottish Rifles (Cameronians) |
| SDF | Sudan Defence Force |
| SEA HIGHRS | Seaforth Highlanders |
| S GDS | Scots Guards |
| SH | Seaforth Highlanders |
| SHROPS LI | Shropshire Light Infantry |
| SHROPS YEO | Shropshire Yeomanry |
| S LAN R | South Lancashire Regiment |
| SLI | Somerset Light Infantry (also SOM LI) |
| S STAFF R | South Staffordshire Regiment |
| SUFF R | Suffolk Regiment |
| SUFF YEO | Suffolk Yeomanry |
| SURR YEO | Surrey Yeomanry |
| SVC | Shanghai Volunteer Corps |
| S WALES BORD | South Wales Borderers |
| WAAC | Women's Auxiliary Army Corps |
| W AFR R | West African Regiment |
| WELSH R | Welsh Regiment |
| WEST & CUMB YEO | Westmoreland & Cumberland Yeomanry |
| W GDS | Welsh Guards |
| WILTS R | Wiltshire Regiment |
| WILTS YEO | Wiltshire Yeomanry |
| WIR | West India Regiment |
| W KENT YEO | West Kent Yeomanry |
| WORC R | Worcestershire Regiment |
| WRAC | Women's Royal Army Corps |

| | |
|---|---|
| W RID R | West Riding Regiment |
| W SOM YEO | West Somerset Yeomanry |
| W YORK R | West Yorkshire Regiment |
| Y & LR | Yorkshire & Lancaster Regiment (also written as YORK & LANC R) |
| YEO | Yeomanry |
| YD | Yorkshire Dragoons (also written as YORK DNS) |
| YH | Yorkshire Hussars (also written as YORK HSRS) |
| YORK R | Yorkshire Regiment |
| YORKS LI | Yorkshire Light Infantry |

*Appendix 3*

# ARMY ABBREVIATIONS – ARMY SERVICE RECORD

This is a very basic list of abbreviations that may appear on a relative's Army service record or in a unit war diary. A far more comprehensive list is supplied by the Record Office in Glasgow when you receive the service record.

| | |
|---|---|
| A | Acting |
| | Assistant |
| AA | Anti-aircraft |
| AA COLL | Army Apprentice College |
| AAI | Allied Army Italy |
| AAS | Army Apprentices School |
| AATS | Anti-aircraft Training School |
| AB | Army Book |
| | Airborne |
| ABC | Armoured Brigade Company (ASC) |
| ABSD | Army Blood Supply Depot (RAMC) |
| ACI | Army Council Instruction |
| AEC | Army Education Company |
| AER | Army Emergency Reserve |
| AF | Army Form |
| AFD | Airborne Forces Depot |
| AFW | Army Field Workshop |
| AG | Adjutant General |
| AGR | Army General Reserve |
| AGRA | Army Group Royal Artillery |
| AIO | Area Intelligence Officer |
| A/L | Air Landing |
| A L/CPL | Acting Lance Corporal |
| AMC | Aerodrome Maintenance Company (RE) |
| AMS | Army Medical Services |
| ANS | Army Nursing Services |
| AOD | Army Ordnance Department |
| | Advanced Ordnance Depot |
| APO | Army Post Office |
| AR | Army Recruiting |

| | |
|---|---|
| ARMD | Armoured |
| ARTY | Artillery |
| ASC | Army Selection Centre |
| ASD | Army Staff Duties |
| A SGT | Acting Sergeant |
| AS OF FH | Army School of Field Hygiene |
| A SURG | Army Surgeon |
| ATC | Armoured Training Centre |
| AT COY | Army Troops Company (RE) |
| ATS | Auxiliary Territorial Service |
| AW | Artisan Works (RE) |
| AWO CL1 | Acting Warrant Officer Class 1 |
| AWOL | Absent Without Leave |
| BANU | British Army News Unit |
| BAPO | British Army Post Office (RE) |
| BC | Battle Casualty |
| BCOF | British Commonwealth Occupation Force (Japan) |
| BD | Bomb Disposal |
| | Base Depot |
| BDC | Bomb Disposal Company |
| BDE | Brigade |
| BDR | Bombardier |
| BDS | Bomb Disposal Section (RE) |
| BDSM | Bandsman |
| BEF | British Expeditionary Force |
| BFBS | British Forces Broadcasting Service |
| BN | Battalion |
| BOD | Base Ordnance Depot |
| BPTC | Bulk Petrol Transport Company (RASC) |
| BQMS | Battery Quartermaster Sergeant |
| BRC | Base Reinforcement Camp |
| BRIG | Brigadier |
| BSD | Base Supply Depot (RASC) |
| BSM | Battery Sergeant Major |
| BTTN | Battalion |
| BTY | Battery |
| CAPT | Captain |
| CCF | Combined Cadet Force |
| CCS | Casualty Clearing Station |
| CG | Chaplain General |
| CGS | Chief of General Staff |
| C-in-C | Commander-in-Chief |
| CIC | Commander-in-Chief |
| | Cookery Instruction Centre |
| | Civilian Internment Camp |
| CMF | Central Mediterranean Force |
| CO | Commanding Officer |
| COD | Central Ordnance Depot |
| COL | Colonel |

| | |
|---|---|
| COMD | Command |
| | Commander |
| COMDT | Commandant |
| COY | Company |
| Cpl | Corporal |
| CQMS | Company Quartermaster Sergeant |
| CSDU | Central Salvage Depot Unit |
| CSEU | Combined Services Entertainment Unit |
| C SGT | Colour Sergeant |
| CSM | Company Sergeant Major |
| CTBA | Ceased to be Attached |
| CW | Chemical Warfare |
| D&T | Development & Training |
| DB | Depot Battalion (RE) |
| | Depot Brigade (RA) |
| DC | District Commander |
| DCM | Distinguished Conduct Medal |
| | District Court Martial |
| DE | Duration of Emergency |
| DID | Detail Issue Depot (RASC) |
| DIV | Division |
| DM | Driver Mechanical Transport (RASC) |
| DMR | Drummer |
| DMS | Driver Mechanical School |
| D OF E | Duration of Engagement |
| D OF W | Duration of War |
| DPM | Deputy Provost Marshal |
| DR | Despatch Rider |
| DSAF | Depot & School Airborne Forces |
| DSO | Distinguished Service Order |
| DVR | Driver |
| E&M Coy | Electrical & Mechanical Company (RE) |
| ECC | Emergency Cooks Course |
| EEF | Egyptian Expeditionary Force |
| EME (A) | Electrical & Mechanical Engineering (Army) |
| ENGR | Engineers |
| ENSA | Entertainment National Service Association |
| ERE | Extra Regimentally Employed |
| ESBD | Electrical Stores Base Depot |
| | Engineer Store Base Depot |
| ESD | Engineer Store Depot |
| ESE | Engineer Store Establishment |
| EST | Establishments |
| FA | Field Ambulance (might be shown as F AMB) |
| FARELF | Far East Land Force |
| F Coy | Fortress Company |
| FDS | Field Dressing Station |
| | Forward Delivery Squadron (RAC) |
| FGCM | Field General Court Martial |

| | |
|---|---|
| FH | Field Hospital |
| FLD BKY | Field Bakery |
| FOU | Forward Observation Unit (RA) |
| FPS | Field Park Squadron (RE) (might also be shown as FPKS |
| FSS | Field Security Section |
| FUS | Fusilier (rank equivalent to Private) |
| FVPE | Fighting Vehicle Proving Establishment |
| FWN | Forewoman (NCO in QMAAC) |
| GC | George Cross |
| GC COY | General Construction Company (RE) |
| GCM | General Court Martial |
| GDSM | Guardsman (rank equivalent to Private in the Guards Regiments) |
| GEN | General |
| GH | General Hospital |
| GM | George Medal |
| Gnr | Gunner (rank equivalent to Private in Royal Artillery) |
| GOC | General Officer Commanding |
| GOC in C | General Officer Commanding in Chief |
| GRO | General Routine Order |
| GS | General Service |
| GSO | General Staff Officer |
| GT COY | General Transport Company |
| GTTB | General Trades Training Battalions (Royal Signals) |
| HAA | Heavy Anti-aircraft |
| HAT | Home Ambulance Train (RAMC) |
| HCBTC | Home Counties Brigade Training Centre |
| HD | Home Defence |
| HPS | Home Port Security (Intelligence Corps) |
| HRS (MT) | Heavy Repair Shop (Motor Transport) |
| HS | Holding Strength |
| | Hospital Ship |
| HSF | Home Service Force |
| HTR | Heavy Training Regiment (RAC) |
| I | Intelligence |
| I/C | In Charge of |
| ICC | Intelligence Corps Centre |
| IE | Inspectorate of Establishments |
| INF | Infantry (may also appear as INFY) |
| ITC | Infantry Training Centre |
| IWP | Instruments and Weapons Production |
| L | Labour |
| LAC | London Assembly Centre |
| LAD | Light Aid Detachment |
| L CPL | Lance Corporal (may also be written L/CPL) |
| LDAC | London District Assembly Centre |
| LDRD | London District Reception Depot (RAC) |
| LDY OP | Laundry Operator (RAOC) |
| LIEUT | Lieutenant (may also be written LT) |
| L OF C | Line of Communications |

| | |
|---|---|
| L SGT | Lance Sergeant |
| LSL | Long Service List |
| LT COL | Lieutenant Colonel |
| LTR | Long Term Reserve |
| LWOP | Leave Without Pay |
| MA | Military Attaché |
| | Military Assistant |
| MAC | Motorised Ambulance Company (RAMC) |
| MAD | Military Accounts Department |
| MAJ | Major |
| MC | Military Cross |
| | Movement Control |
| | Motor Cycle |
| MCU | Military Collection Unit |
| MDC | Mobile Defence Company |
| MD COY | Motor Driver Company (ATS) |
| ME COY | Mechanical Equipment Company |
| MEF | Mediterranean Expeditionary Force |
| MELF | Middle East Land Force |
| MEP | Mechanical Equipment Park Company (RE) |
| MEXE | Military Engineering Experimental Establishment |
| MIRC | Military Intelligence Research Centre |
| MLU | Mobile Laundry Unit (RAOC) |
| MM | Military Medal |
| MO | Medical Officer |
| MOB | Mobilisation |
| MOV | Movement |
| MP&DB | Military Prison & Detention Barracks |
| MPDB | Military Provost Detention Barracks |
| MPFS | Mobile Petrol Filling Station |
| MPTC | Mobile Petrol Transport Company |
| MRS | Medical Reception Station |
| MSD | Main Supply Depot (RAOC) |
| MSG | Maintenance Support Group |
| MT | Mechanical Transport |
| MT BN | Motor Training Battalion |
| MTO | Mechanical Transport Officer |
| MTS | Motor Transport Stores |
| MTTD | Motor Transport Training Depot |
| MWEE | Mechanical Warfare Experimental Establishment |
| NAAFI | Navy, Army and Air Force Institutes |
| NCO | Non-commissioned officer |
| NID | North Irish Depot |
| NO | Nursing Orderly |
| NSRW | National Service Reserve Wing |
| OAC | Ordnance Ammunition Company |
| OC | Officer Commanding |
| OCA | Old Comrades Association |
| OCTU | Officer Cadet Training Unit |

| | |
|---|---|
| OFC | Operator Fire Control (RA) |
| OFP | Ordnance Field Park |
| OIC | Officer in Charge |
| OPWC | Overseas Prisoner of War Camp |
| ORD | Ordnance |
| OTC | Officer Training Corps |
| PCC | Port Construction Company |
| PCLU | Pioneer & Civil Labour Unit |
| PD | Petrol Depot |
| P/M | Pipe Major |
| PM | Provost Marshal |
| PMR | Paymaster |
| | Practical Map Reading |
| PNE | Permanently Non Effective |
| POC | Port Operating Company |
| POW | Prisoner of War |
| P PARK | Petrol Park |
| PSM | Platoon Sergeant Major |
| PSP | Petrol Stores Platoon |
| PTC | Primary Training Corps |
| Pte | Private |
| PTFOC | Petrol Tin Factory Operating Company (RASC) |
| PTW | Primary Training Wing |
| PVO | Principal Veterinary Officer |
| Q | Quartering |
| QM | Quartermaster |
| QMG | Quartermaster General |
| QMS | Quartermaster Sergeant |
| RB | Reinforcement Base |
| RC COY | Railway Construction Company (RE) |
| RCM | Regimental Court Martial |
| RDD | Reception and Discharge Depot |
| REGT | Regiment |
| RFN | Rifleman (rank equivalent to Private) |
| RHE | Returned to Home Establishment |
| RMAS | Royal Military Academy, Sandhurst |
| RMC | Royal Military College |
| RMO | Regimental Medical Officer |
| RMW | Railway Mobile Workshop |
| RO | Recruiting Officer |
| RQMS | Regimental Quartermaster Sergeant |
| RSC | Recruit Selection Centre |
| RTO | Railway Transportation Office (Officer) |
| SA SCHOOL | Small Arms School (also written S ARMS SCH) |
| SCD | Stores and Clothing Department |
| SCU | Special Communications Unit |
| SEAC | South East Asia Command |
| SEALF | South East Asia Land Force |
| SGT | Sergeant |

| | |
|---|---|
| SIB | Special Investigations Branch |
| SIG | Signalman (rank equivalent to Private) |
| SL | Searchlight |
| SM | Sergeant Major (also written S MJR) |
| SME | School of Mechanical Engineering |
| SNLR | Services No Longer Required |
| SOE | Special Operations Executive |
| S OF M | School of Musketry |
| SOS | Struck Off Strength |
| Spr | Sapper (rank equivalent to Private) |
| SR | Special Reserve |
| | Supplementary Reserve |
| SRD | Supply Reserve Depot |
| ST | Supply and Transport |
| STC | Survey Training Centre |
| SU | Salvage Unit |
| SVY | Survey |
| TA | Territorial Army |
| TAVR | Territorial Army Volunteer Reserve |
| TB | Training Battalion |
| | Tank Brigade |
| TCC | Traffic Control Company |
| TE | Training Establishment |
| TN | Transportation |
| TOS | Taken On Strength |
| TP CG COY | Troop Carrying Company (RASC) |
| TPR | Trooper |
| TRG | Training |
| VAD | Voluntary Aid Detachment |
| VC | Victoria Cross |
| VCP | Vehicle Collection Point |
| VD | Venereal Disease |
| VPP | Vulnerable Points Provost (Military Police) |
| VRD | Vehicle Reserve Depot |
| W or W/S | War Substantive (of a rank) |
| WE | War Establishment |
| WEF | With Effect From |
| WI | Wireless Intelligence |
| WKR | Worker (equivalent to Private in QMAAC) |
| WO | War Office |
| | Warrant Officer |
| WO CL 1 | Warrant Officer Class 1 |
| YEO | Yeomanry |
| YS | Young Soldier |

# *Appendix 4*

# ROYAL AIR FORCE ACRONYMS

As a technical service the RAF used hundreds of acronyms in its documentation and some, at least, will appear in every man or woman's service record, log book or other documentation. This is not a comprehensive list but hopefully it will provide ideas to help you search out an individual's postings, the nature of their work or their medical condition.

| | |
|---|---|
| AAC | Army Air Corps |
| AAEE | Aeroplane and Armament Experimental Establishment |
| AAF | Auxiliary Air Force |
| A&GS | Armament & Gunnery School |
| A&IC Sch | Artillery & Infantry Cooperation School |
| A/C | Aircraft |
| ACC | Army Co-operation Command |
| ACDW | Air Crew Disposal Wing |
| ACHU | Aircrew Holding Unit |
| ACMB | Aviation Candidates Medical Board |
| ACRC | Air Crew Reception Centre |
| ACSB | Air Crew Selection Board |
| AD | Aircraft Depot |
| ADGB | Air Defence of Great Britain |
| ADRU | Air Despatch & Reception Unit |
| ADU | Aircraft Delivery Unit |
| AED | Aircraft Equipment Depot |
| AF | Advanced Flying/Air Fighting |
| AFE | Airborne Forces Establishment |
| AFEE | Airborne Forces Experimental Establishment |
| AFS | Auxiliary Fighter Squadron |
| AGBS | Air Gunnery & Bombing School |
| AGRS | Advanced Ground Radio School |
| Air Min/AM | Air Ministry |
| ALG | Advance Landing Ground |
| ALO | Air Liaison Officer |
| ANBS | Air Navigation & Bombing School |
| AO | Air Observer |
| AOC | Air Officer Commanding |

| | |
|---|---|
| AOP | Air Observation Post |
| AP | Aircraft |
| ARC | Aircrew Recruiting Centre |
| | Aircrew Reception Centre |
| ARD/F | Aircraft Repair Depot/Flight |
| ARP/S/U | Aircraft/Aeroplane Repair Park/Section/Unit |
| A/S | Anti Submarine |
| AS&RU | Aircraft Salvage & Repair Unit |
| ASC | Aircrew Selection Centre |
| ASD | Aeroplane Supply Depot |
| ASP | Air Stores Park |
| ASR | Air Sea Rescue |
| ASS | Air Signals School |
| ASU | Aircraft Storage Unit |
| ATA | Air Transport Auxiliary |
| ATC | Air Traffic Control |
| | Air Training Corps |
| ATFERO | Atlantic Ferry Organisation |
| ATS | Auxiliary Territorial Service (Women) |
| | Armament Training Station |
| | Air Training Squadron |
| AWF | All Weather Flight |
| AWOL | Absent Without Leave |
| B&C | Barrack & Clothing |
| B&GS | Bombing & Gunnery School |
| BANS | Basic Air Navigation School |
| BBOC | Brought Back on Charge (applies to repaired aircraft) |
| BC | Bomber Command |
| BCAS | Bomber Command Armament School |
| BCATP | British Commonwealth Air Training Plan |
| BCBS | Bomber Command Bombing School |
| BCMC | Bomber Command Modification Centre |
| BDU | Bomb Disposal Unit |
| BER | Beyond Economical Repair |
| BMH | British Military Hospital |
| BRD | Base Repair Depot |
| BSDU | Bomber Support Development Unit |
| BTU | Bombing Trials Unit |
| BU | Broken Up |
| (C) | Coastal |
| CACF | Coast Artillery Co-operation Flight |
| CAEU | Casualty Air Evacuation Unit |
| C&M | Care and Maintenance |
| Cam-ship | Catapult-armed Merchantship |
| CARD | Central Aircraft Repair Depot |
| Casevac | Casualty Evacuation |
| CBCF/S | Coastal Battery Cooperation Flight/School |
| CC | Confined to Camp |
| CCFATU | Coastal Command Fighter Affiliation & Training Unit |

| | |
|---|---|
| CF | Communication Flight |
| | Conversion Flight |
| (C)FPP | Civilian Ferry Pilots Pool |
| CF(S) | Communications Flight (Squadron) |
| CFS | Central Flying School |
| CF/Unit | Camouflage Flight/Unit |
| CGIS | Central Gliding Instructors School |
| CGS | Central Gunnery School |
| | Central Gliding School |
| Cmd | Command |
| CMU | Civilian Maintenance Unit |
| CNS | Central Navigation School |
| CO | Commanding Officer (can also be OC) |
| Comm(s) | Communication(s) |
| Conv | Conversion |
| CPE | Central Photographic Establishment |
| CRE | Central Reconnaissance Establishment |
| CRO | Civilian Repair Organisation |
| CRP | Civilian Repair Party |
| CS | Communication Squadron |
| Cse | Course |
| CSE | Central Signals Establishment |
| CSF/S | Communications and Support Flight/Squadron |
| CTS | Combat Training School |
| CU | Conversion Unit |
| CW | Communication Wing |
| DAF | Desert Air Force |
| DBF | Destroyed by Fire (applies to aircraft) |
| DBR | Damaged Beyond Repair (applies to aircraft) |
| Del/Dly | Delivery |
| Det/Dett | Detachment (detachment to another unit or squadron) |
| DI | Daily Inspection |
| Disb | Disbanded |
| DU | Development Unit |
| E/A | Enemy Aircraft |
| EAAS/NS | Empire Air Armament School/ Navigation School |
| EAOS | Elementary Air Observer School |
| EATS | Empire Air Training Scheme |
| EDD | Equipment Disposal Unit |
| EFTS | Elementary Flying Training School |
| EGS | Elementary Gliding School |
| ELG | Emergency Landing Ground |
| EOWS | Elementary Observer Wireless School |
| EPD | Equipment & Personnel Depot |
| ERS | Empire Radio School |
| | Engine Repair Section |
| ETPS | Empire Test Pilots School |
| EU | Equipment Unit |
| Evd | Evaded Capture |

| | |
|---|---|
| FAA | Fleet Air Arm |
| FAGS | Fleet Aerial Gunners School |
| FBDF/SU | Flying Boat Development Flight/ Servicing Unit |
| FC | Ferry Command |
| | Fighter Command |
| | Flying Control |
| FCCS/F | Fighter Command Communication Squadron/Flight |
| FCITF/S | Fighter Command Instrument Training Flight/Squadron |
| FCPU | Ferry Command Preparation Unit |
| FCRS | Fighter Command Radar School |
| FCTU | Fighter Command Trials Unit |
| F/E | Flight Engineer |
| FE | Far East |
| FECEU | Far East Casualty Evacuation Unit |
| FEE | Fighter Experimental Establishment |
| FEFBW | Far East Flying Boat Wing |
| FFI | Free From Infection |
| FIS | Flying Instructors School |
| FLS | Fighter Leaders School |
| Flt | Flight |
| FPP | Ferry Pilots Pool |
| FR | Fighter-reconnaissance |
| FRD | Forward Repair Depot |
| FRU | Field Repair Unit |
| FS | Fighting School |
| FSAF&G | Fleet School of Aerial Fighting & Gunnery |
| FSS | Ferry Support Squadron |
| | Flying Selection Squadron |
| FTC | Flying Training Command |
| FTR | Failed to Return |
| FU | Ferry Unit |
| G | Glider |
| | Gliding |
| GATU | Ground Attack Training Unit |
| GC | Gliding Centre |
| GD | General Duties |
| GDC | Group Disbandment Centre |
| GED | Ground Equipment Depot |
| GES | Glider Exercise Squadron |
| GG | Ground Gunnery |
| GI | Ground Instructional |
| GIF | Glider Instructors Flight |
| Gp | Group |
| GPR | Glider Pilot Regiment |
| GPUTU | Glider Pick-up Training Unit |
| GRSS | Ground Radio Servicing Squadron |
| GRU/F | General Reconnaissance Unit/Flight |
| GSE | Glider Servicing Echelon |
| GTF | Gunnery Training Flight |

| | |
|---|---|
| GTPS | Glider & Tug Pilots School |
| GTS | Glider Training Squadron/Glider Training School |
| HAD | Home Aircraft Depot |
| (HB) | Heavy Bomber |
| HCCS | Home Command Communications Squadron |
| HCF | Home Communications Flight |
| HE | Home Establishment |
| HFF | Heavy Freight Flight |
| HFU | Home Ferry Unit |
| HG | Heavy Glider |
| Hosp | Hospital |
| HS Flt | High Speed Flight |
| HT | Heavy Transport |
| (I) | India |
| IAAD | Inland Area Aircraft Depot |
| IAF | Indian Air Force |
| i/c | In Charge |
| IFDU | Intensive Flying Development Unit |
| IFF | Identification Friend or Foe |
| IFTS | Initial Flying Training School |
| Int | Interned |
| I/O | Intelligence Officer |
| IR | Immediate Reserve |
| ISF | Internal Security Flight |
| IT | Initial Training |
| JAPIC | Joint Air Photographic Interpretation Centre |
| JARIC | Joint Air Reconnaissance Intelligence Centre |
| JCU | Jet Conversion Unit |
| JEHU | Joint Experimental Helicopter Unit |
| JHDU | Joint Helicopter Development Unit |
| JTF | Jet Training Flight |
| JSPI | Joint School of Photographic Interpretation |
| JSSC | Joint Services Staff College |
| JSTU | Joint Services Trials Unit |
| KF | King's Flight |
| KRs | King's Regulations |
| LAAGS | Light Anti-aircraft Gunnery School |
| LAS | Light Aircraft School |
| LG | Landing Ground |
| LLF | Light Liaison Flight |
| LRDF | Long Range Development Flight |
| LRFU | Long Range Ferry Unit |
| LRWRE | Long Range Weapons Research Establishment |
| MA | Marine Aircraft |
| MAC | Mediterranean Air Command |
| M&D | Medicine and Duties |
| MAD | Marine Acceptance Depot |
| MAP | Ministry of Aircraft Production |
| MASR&CF | Malta Air Sea Rescue & Communications Flight |

| | |
|---|---|
| MATAF | Mediterranean Allied Tactical Air Forces |
| MC | Maintenance Command |
| MCA | Ministry of Civil Aviation |
| ME | Middle East |
| MED | Medical Equipment Depot |
| Med Dist | Mediterranean District |
| MEP&AP | Middle East Pilot & Aircrew Pool |
| Met Res | Meteorological Research |
| MF | Meteorological Flight |
| MFPU | Mobile Field Photographic Unit |
| MGSP | Mobile Glider Servicing Party |
| MO | Medical Officer |
| MOA | Ministry of Aviation |
| MORU | Mobile Operations Room Unit |
| MOS | Marine Observation School |
| MRS | Maritime Recognisance School |
| MRU | Medical Rehabilitation Unit |
| MT | Motor Transport |
| MTDpt | Marine Training Depot |
| MTE | Medical Training Establishment |
| MTLRU | Motor Transport Light Repair Unit |
| MU | Maintenance Unit |
| Nav | Navigator |
| Navex | Navigation Exercise |
| NCU | Night Conversion Unit |
| N/E | Non Effective |
| NFDS/W/U | Night Fighter Development Squadron/Wing/Unit |
| NFF | Night Fighter Flight |
| NFT | Night Flying Test |
| NFTS | Night Fighter Training Squadron |
| NICF | Night Conversion Flight |
| NTS | Night Training Squadron |
| NVTS | Night Vision Training School |
| (O) | Observer |
| OADF/U | Overseas Aircraft Delivery Flight/Unit |
| OANS | Observers Air Navigation School |
| OAPU | Overseas Aircraft Preparation Unit |
| OATS | Officers Advanced Training School |
| Obs Sch/OBS | Observer School |
| OCU | Operational Conversion Unit |
| OEU | Operational Evaluation Unit |
| OFU | Overseas Ferry Unit |
| OP | Observation Post (Army Air Corps Unit) |
| Opl | Operational |
| ORTU | Operational & Refresher Training Unit |
| OS | Observers School |
| OSR&AG | Observers School of Reconnaissance & Aerial Gunnery |
| OTU | Operational Training Unit |
| OTTW | Officer's Technical Training Wing |

| | |
|---|---|
| (P) | Pilot |
| PACT | Pre Aircrew Training |
| PD | Packing Depot |
| PDC | Personnel Dispersal Centre |
| PDRC | Personnel Despatch and Reception Centre |
| PDU | Personnel Dispersal Unit |
| | Photographic Development Unit |
| PF | Practice Flight |
| PFF | Pathfinder Force |
| PGTS | Parachute & Glider Training School |
| PHU | Personnel Holding Unit |
| PIU | Photographic Intelligence Unit |
| POW | Prisoner of War |
| PPF | Parachute Practice Flight |
| PPP | Pupils Pilots Pool |
| PR | Photographic Reconnaissance |
| PRC | Personnel Reception Centre |
| PRDU/E | Photographic Reconnaissance Development Unit/ Establishment |
| PRFU/S | Pilots Refresher Flying Unit/School |
| PRU | Personnel Reception Unit |
| PRU | Photographic Reconnaissance Unit |
| | Pilot Replacement Unit |
| PS | Parachute School |
| PTC | Parachute Training Centre |
| | Personnel Transit Camp |
| PTF | Parachute Test Flight |
| PTU | Parachute Test Unit |
| | Parachute Training Unit |
| PTU&RP | Pilots Training Unit & Reinforcement Pool |
| QF | Queen's Flight |
| QFI | Qualified Flying Instructor |
| QRs | Queen's Regulations |
| (R) | Reserve |
| RAAF | Royal Australian Air Force |
| | Royal Auxiliary Air Force |
| RAE | Royal Aircraft/Aerospace Establishment |
| RAFC | Royal Air Force College |
| RAFFC | Royal Air Force Flying College |
| RAFG | Royal Air Force Germany |
| RAFR | Royal Air Force Regiment |
| RAFSC | Royal Air Force Staff College |
| RAFVR | Royal Air Force Volunteer Reserve |
| RAP | Reserve Aircraft Pool |
| RAS | Reserve Aeroplane Squadron |
| R&SS | Repair & Salvage Section |
| RC | Reception Centre |
| | Recruit Centre |
| | Reserve Command |
| RCAF | Royal Canadian Air Force |

| | |
|---|---|
| RDUK | Repairable at Depot in UK |
| REC | Release Embarkation Centre |
| Recce | Reconnaissance |
| RFF/U | Refresher Flying Flight/Unit |
| RFS | Reserve Flying School |
| R/G | Rear Gunner |
| RMU | Radio Maintenance Unit |
| RNAS | Royal Naval Air Station |
| RNEFTS | Royal Navy Elementary Flying Training School |
| ROC | Royal Observer Corps |
| ROS | Repairable on Site (of aircraft) |
| RRF(U) | Radio Reconnaissance Flight (Unit) |
| RS | Radio School |
| | Reserve School |
| | Reserve Squadron |
| RSU | Repair & Servicing Unit |
| | Repair and Salvage Unit |
| R/T | Radio Telegraphy |
| | Radio Telephony |
| RTP | Recruit Training Pool |
| RTU | Return To Unit |
| RU | Reception Unit (of people) |
| | Repair Unit (of aircraft) |
| RWE | Radio Warfare Establishment |
| S/Sch | School |
| SA | South African |
| SAR | Search & Rescue |
| SAS | Servicing Aircraft Section |
| S&TT | Station & Target Towing |
| SC | Salvage Centre |
| SCR | School of Control & Reporting |
| SCS | Special Communication Squadron |
| SD | Special Duty |
| | Special Duties |
| | Stores Depot |
| SDU | Signals Development Unit |
| S/E | Single Engined |
| SEAC | South East Asia Command |
| SFTS | Service Flying Training School |
| SGR | School of General Reconnaissance |
| SHAEF | Supreme Headquarters Allied Expeditionary Force |
| Sigs | Signals |
| SIU | Signals Intelligence Unit |
| S/L | Searchlights |
| SL | Sick Leave |
| SLG | Satellite Landing Ground |
| SMR | School of Maritime Reconnaissance |
| SNBD | School of Aerial Navigation and Bomb Dropping |
| SNC | School of Naval Cooperation |

| | |
|---|---|
| SOC | Struck Off Charge (of aircraft) |
| SOF | Special Operations Flight |
| SofFP | School of Fighter Plotting |
| SofP | School of Photography |
| SoN&BD | School of Navigation & Bomb Dropping |
| SoNC&AN | School of Naval Cooperation & Aerial Navigation |
| SoSF | School of Special Flying |
| SPTU | Staff Pilots Training Unit |
| Sq/Sqn/Sqd | Squadron |
| SR | Strategic Reconnaissance |
| SRCU | Short Range Conversion Unit |
| SROs | Station Routine Orders |
| SRTS | Short Range Transport Squadron |
| SRU/W | Strategic Reconnaissance Unit/Wing |
| SS | Signals School |
| | Salvage Section |
| SSF | Special Service Flight |
| | Special Survey Flight |
| Stn | Station |
| STS | Seaplane Training Squadron |
| SU | Support Unit |
| | Servicing Unit |
| Supy | Supernumary |
| SWTS | Supplementary Wireless Telegraphy School |
| T | Training |
| | Transmitter |
| TA | Transport Aircraft |
| TAF | Tactical Air Force |
| TAG | Telegraphist Air Gunner (Fleet Air Arm) |
| TB | Torpedo Bomber |
| TC | Training Command |
| | Transport Command |
| TCAEU | Transport Command Aircrew Examining Unit |
| TCICU | Transport Command Initial Conversion Unit |
| TEE | Test & Evaluation Establishment |
| TF | Training Flight |
| TFP | Training Ferry Pool |
| TFPP | Temporary Ferry Pilots Pool |
| | Training Ferry Pilots School |
| TFU | Telecommunications Flying Unit |
| TPO | Teleprinter Operator |
| TPS | Test Pilots School |
| T/R | Transmitter/Receiver |
| Trg | Training |
| TS | Training School |
| | Training Squadron |
| TSCU | Transport Support Conversion Unit |
| TSR | Torpedo Spotter reconnaissance |
| TSTS | Trade Selection Test Section |

| | |
|---|---|
| TT | Target Towing |
| | Trade Training |
| TTC | Technical Training Command |
| TTS | Torpedo Training School/Squadron |
| TTU | Torpedo Training Unit |
| | Target Towing Unit |
| TU | Training Unit |
| UAS | University Air Squadron |
| UED | Universal Equipment Depot |
| u/i | Unidentified |
| us | Unserviceable |
| USAAC/F | United States Army Air Corps/Force |
| W or Wg | Wing |
| WAAF | Women's Auxiliary Air Force |
| W&OS | Wireless & Observers School |
| WEE | Wireless Experimental Establishment |
| WIDU | Wireless Intelligence Development Unit |
| W/Op | Wireless Operator |
| WOp/AG | Wireless Operator/Air Gunner |
| WRAF | Women's Royal Air Force |
| WRAFVR (T) | Women's Royal Air Force Volunteer Reserve (Training Branch) |
| WS | Wireless School |
| WT | Wireless Telegraphy |
| | Wireless Telephony |

*Appendix 5*

# WEBSITES

There are a huge number of websites dedicated to aspects of the Second World War, some of extremely high quality, others rather more dubious. This is a purely personal list of sites that you might find useful, of sites that I've used regularly or that are either official or otherwise important.

One good thing about the Internet is that it allows publication of locally researched material on places and individuals which might never have been published in books. It's well worth searching for information on, for example, local Home Guard units or bombing raids in which an ancestor was killed or injured. Examples of these types of site include: http://www .walescottages.com/auxiliary_hideout.htm, which looks at an Auxiliary Unit base in South Wales, http://www.exetermemories.co.uk/em/blitzcasual-ties.php, which lists casualties of the nineteen German air raids on the city of Exeter, and http://www.staffshomeguard.co.uk, an excellent site relating to the Staffordshire Home Guard. There are thousands of such sites, with more being added almost daily, so a good search around may prove interesting and invaluable. You may even care to share your own researches by creating a website yourself.

TNA website is at: http://www.nationalarchives.gov.uk and is probably the first and most important website that you'll need to look at and understand. Holding over 1,000 years of government documents it's inevitable that every family historian will have cause to visit TNA, either in person or through their growing collection of documents available online.

Their catalogue at: http://www.nationalarchives.gov.uk/catalogue allows a range of search facilities, both complex and simple – but remember, it only searches on file descriptions, not on contents, so a certain amount of background knowledge about your subject, the service they were in, when they served, what squadron/ship/regiment etc. is required to make the best of it. By all means try searching first on their name as some occasional surprises come up – I found information on my mysterious great-great uncle Valentine Tomaselli simply by typing in his name. But be warned – when individuals are found like this it's usually because they've been in court, involved in a divorce or otherwise come to the government's attention for the wrong reasons.

Some Second World War records are available online through TNA's website, including 'Recommendations for Honours and Awards' (TNA's WO

373 series), 'Royal Naval Officers Service Records' (from ADM 196, which includes records of more senior officers in the Navy during the Second World War), 'Second World War Merchant Shipping Movement Cards' (BT 389) and 'Air Combat Reports, Second World War' (AIR 50). Further additions are always being made so it's worth checking the DocumentsOnline section of the website regularly.

Army Museums, Ogilvie Trust is a registered charity that assists military museums, with a website at: http://www.armymuseums.org.uk. The site allows you to search for regimental and corps museums that may have useful information. Once located, the site gives links to the museum's website, details of its location and facilities.

The National Army Museum website is at: http://www.national-army-museum.ac.uk. It's the museum of the Army as a whole. Its collection includes a large number of regimental and campaign histories, archives, photographs, prints and drawings, providing a rich picture of soldiers' daily lives through the ages.

There is an excellent web site dealing with the general history of the Home Guard at: http://www.home-guard.org.uk.

Basic research on servicemen and Merchant Seamen killed during the Second World War can be carried out through the website of the Commonwealth War Graves Commission at: http://www.cwgc.org. You can search for a deceased relative using their name and discover when they died and where they are buried or otherwise commemorated, with usually some brief detail of their family.

The Imperial War Museum at: www.iwm.org.uk has extensive collections of official photographs, sound archives of recollections of veterans and a huge library, a somewhat daunting (at first) search engine for their extensive collections of material and some useful links for family historians.

A huge website devoted to military history generally, with much information on the Second World War is at: http://www.historyofwar .org/index.html. Among many other interesting features it has a day-by-day timeline of the Second World War at: http://www.historyofwar.org/second-worldwar/date/index.html, which allows you to look at specific dates. The information is quite high level but may offer clues to what was going on in a particular theatre of the war while your ancestor was serving there.

http://www.ww2cemeteries.co.uk records details of every Second World War war cemetery in Europe, and provides links to many other fascinating sites and basic information on researching Second World War soldiers.

http://www.ww2battlefields.info provides useful information on Second World War battlefields in Europe, Orders of Battle, more useful links and advice.

The BBC website at: http://www.bbc.co.uk/ww2peopleswar contains 47,000 stories of the war recounted by members of the public between June 2003 and January 2006. Though unmediated, so that they hardly count as academic sources, they are frequently vivid and give an idea of events as seen from the bottom up. They cover all aspects of the war and are well worth a look.

The Royal Air Force official website at; http://www.raf.mod.uk provides a comprehensive history of the service through its link with the RAF Historical Branch, including a timeline of RAF events and accounts of RAF squadrons. This site has been under redevelopment for as long as I can remember so don't be surprised to find yourself being redirected.

An excellent private site dedicated to RAF Bomber Command at: www.bomber-command.info provides much interesting and useful information on Bomber Command's war.

The Royal Air Force Museum website is at: http://www.rafmusem.org.uk. For family history research click on the Hendon section and then 'Research'. This takes you through to the Department of Research and Information Services (DoRIS) where you can find out how to arrange a visit to the archive, some basic information on the types of records kept and how to locate individuals' service records. There is a 'Frequently Asked Questions' section. The Museum's collections 'Online Navigator' contains a selection of records relating to items in the collection. It is not a complete catalogue of the Museum's holdings but allows you to search their database and find out more about their collection.

There is a huge amount of information on the RAF in the Second World War at: http://www.rafcommands.com. Their Forum provides answers to questions and their members have a wide range of knowledge.

http://www.airtransportaux.com is an excellent site devoted to the ATA with sections on its history, some articles on the subject and photographs.

The Royal Naval Museum site at: http://www.royalnavalmuseum.org contains details of their extensive collections of naval material with a search facility. There is also a large selection of material viewable online in their 'Sea Your History' section, including thousands of photographs.

The official site of the Fleet Air Arm is at: http://www.fleetairarm.com. Its archive includes a range of documents related to the Royal Naval Air Service and the Fleet Air Arm, from official and private sources. It covers naval aircraft, personnel, air stations, operations, ships and equipment.

The Fleet Air Arm Archive 1939–45 at: www.fleetairarmarchive.net (please note this is **not** the official site of the Fleet Air Arm Museum) gives many details of FAA units and actions during the Second World War. It has extensive links to other Fleet Air Arm-related sites and a good deal of information on the FAA squadrons, aircraft and personnel.

The Royal Navy Submarine Museum's website is at: http://www .rnsubmus.co.uk and gives details of opening times, how to get there, special events and the Museum collections.

There's a concise history of the submarine service and a complete list of submarine losses, with brief descriptions of the circumstances of their loss at: http://www.rnsubmus.co.uk/general/losses.htm#a1.

The Royal Tank Regiment and Tank Corps Museum website is at: http://www.tankmuseum.co.uk Their archive is internationally recognised and at: http://www.tankmuseum.org/Archive_and_Reference_Library you can find more details of their holdings and how to access them.

Sites of particular interest to researchers into the Home Guard Auxiliary Units are at: http://www.auxunit.org.uk and http://www.parhamairfield museum.co.uk/brohome.html, though there are other sites dealing with local groups. A site dedicated to Coleshill House, the HQ of the units, is currently being revamped and, at the time of writing, hopes to be back online at a new address very soon.

http://www.mariners-l.co.uk provides lots of information on how to research individual ships and Merchant Marine sailors.

http://www.photoship.co.uk is an excellent private website containing photographs of many Second World War period merchant ships.

http://www.uboat.net/index.html is an extremely useful website devoted to German U-boats, detailing the ships they sank during the course of the war. It also gives a great deal of information on the convoys merchant ships sailed in.

An incredibly powerful tool for finding information about people who served in the Australian armed forces during the Second World War is at: http://www.ww2roll.gov.au, a searchable nominal roll that provides basic details of their career. It's searchable using their name and service number.

# BIBLIOGRAPHY

Thousands of books have been published about the Second World War, ranging from general and specific campaign histories, unit histories and personal memoirs, so that it is impossible to give a full and fair bibliography. The following are books I have referred to during various researches or have particularly enjoyed or found useful. Use your local library, or the inter-library loans system, to get hold of them and use their bibliographies as the basis for further research. Please remember that older histories written before about 1975 do not properly take into account the role of Britain's code-breakers and intelligence services in obtaining vital information about the enemy.

## Books Specific to Tracing Ancestors

Brooks, Richard. *Tracing Your Royal Marine Ancestors*, Pen & Sword, 2008
Burton, Anthony. *Tracing Your Shipbuilding Ancestors*, Pen & Sword, 2010
Drummond, Di. *Tracing Your Railway Ancestors*, Pen & Sword, 2010
Fowler, Simon. *Tracing Your Army Ancestors*, Pen & Sword, 2006
—. *Tracing Your Second World War Ancestors*, Countryside Books, 2006
—. *Tracing Your Naval Ancestors*, Pen & Sword, forthcoming
Pappalardo, Bruno. *Tracing Your Naval Ancestors – Public Records Reader's Guide 24*, PRO Publications, 2003
Tomaselli, Phil. *Tracing Your Air Force Ancestors*, Pen & Sword, 2007
—. *Tracing Your Secret Service Ancestors*, Pen & Sword, 2009
Wade, Stephen. *Tracing Your Police Ancestors*, Pen & Sword, 2009
Watts, Christopher T and Michael J. *My Ancestor was a Merchant Seaman*, Society of Genealogists Enterprises, 2004

## The Second World War Generally

Hook, Alex. *World War II Day by Day*, Grange Books, 2004; gives brief summaries of events on a daily basis
Keegan, John. *The Second World War*, Vintage, 1997; covers the main events of the war in a scholarly but readable fashion
Spencer, William. *Medals – The Researcher's Guide*, TNA, 2006

*The Second World War: A Guide to Documents in the Public Records Office*, PRO Handbook No. 15, revd edn 1998; an invaluable guide to the huge holdings of material at TNA

## The Royal Navy

Barnett, Correlli. *Engage the Enemy More Closely*, Hodder & Stoughton, 1991; covers the Royal Navy during the whole of the Second World War and explains clearly the importance of the war at sea

Williams, Andrew. *The Battle of the Atlantic*, BBC Books, 2002; accompanied the excellent TV series of the same name and is well researched with lots of individual reminiscences

## The Army and Campaigns

Barr, Niall. *The Pendulum of War*, Jonathan Cape, 2004; the story of 8th Army in 1942 and how it learnt to defeat the Afrika Corps

Lamb, Richard. *The War in Italy – A Brutal Story*, John Murray, 1993; covers the Italian front from the initial invasion of Sicily in 1943 to the crossing of the Alps into Austria in the final days of the war

MacDonald Fraser, George. *Quartered Safe Out Here*, paperback edn, Harper Collins, 2000; the best book about the war in Burma from the perspective of an ordinary soldier – and one of the best books about an ordinary soldier's experiences of the war

Strawson, John. *The Battle for North Africa*, new edn, Pen & Sword Military Classics, 2004; a good history of the Desert War

## The Royal Air Force

Bungay, Stephen. *The Most dangerous Enemy – A History of the Battle of Britain*, Arum Press, 2000

Chorley, W R. *Bomber Command Losses of the Second World War*, 5 vols, Midland Counties Publishing, 1992–8; the brutal statistics of Bomber Command's war

Fowler, Simon, Elliott, Peter, Conyers Nesbit, Roy and Goulter, Christina. *RAF Records in the PRO – PRO Readers' Guide 8*, PRO Publications, 1994

Middlebrook, Martin and Everit, Chris. *The Bomber Command War Diaries – An Operational Reference Book*, Viking, 1985; details every raid carried out by Bomber Command during the war, though, sadly, individual squadrons are rarely mentioned. It does give a good idea of the sheer scale of Bomber Command's war

Shores, C and Williams, C. *Aces High*, Grub Street, 1994; the definitive details of British and Commonwealth fighter aces in the Second World War

Terraine, John. *The Right of the Line – The RAF in the European War 1939–1945*, Hodder & Stoughton, 1985

## Secret Organisations

Cocks, Albert. *Churchill's Secret Army*, Book Guild, 1992; the autobiography of an auxiliary patrol member

Hinsley, F H. *British Intelligence in the Second World War*, abridged edn, HMSO, 1993

Lampe, John. *The Last Ditch*, Cassell, 1969; the first history of the auxiliary units

Oxenden, Major N V. 'Auxiliary Units – History and Achievement'; a booklet written by Major Oxenden, an AU Intelligence officer in October 1944 and republished by the Parnham Museum

Warwicker, John. *With Britain in Mortal Danger*, Cerberus Publishing, 2002; explores the role of the British resistance units and other connected clandestine bodies

## The Home Front

Barker, Rachel. *Conscience, Government and War: Conscientious Objection in Great Britain, 1939–1945*, Routledge & Kegan Paul, 1982

MacKenzie, S P. *The Home Guard*, OUP, 1995; a general history of the Home Guard but its bibliography lists forty-five unit histories from platoon to battalion level

Taylor, Warwick. *The Forgotten Conscript – A History of the Bevin Boys*, Pentland Press, 1995

*The Blitz Then and Now*, Battle of Britain Prints International Ltd, 1987, 1988, 1990); a three-part chronological history of German air raids on Britain with sufficient detail on each raid to get a researcher started, lots of contemporary photographs and personal accounts, as well as recent photographs of the same sites

# INDEX